TRUE BELIEVER

The Journey of Kelly Codling

Entrepreneurship, Struggles, Victories, Life,
Love, Heart Family, All That Good Stuff

"I want to inspire. It's not about money.
It's about heart. It's about perseverance."

"Working for yourself is the best medicine."

Bilbo Books Publishing

ATHENS, GEORGIA

TRUE BELIEVER: THE STORY OF KELLY CODLING

Bilbo Books Publishing
www.BilboBooks.com

ISBN- 978-0-9981627-0-6
ISBN- 0-9981627-1-X
Printed in the United States of America

To my grandmother, Rosetta Codling,
who inspired me to become a True Believer
&
my mother, Amy Codling,
who made me the man I am

To. Don a Very, Very good
Friend for 20 or more years
Also a Very good Customer

Relly Codling
6/2/80

INTRODUCTION

I run a restaurant, two of them actually, and I'm a happy man. My name is Kelbourne "Kelly" Codling, and if you live in Athens, Georgia and have eaten Jamaican food in this town, it's a safe bet that it came from one of my restaurants.

I wanted to write this book to tell my personal story, but, more than that, to inspire others to follow their dreams, to never give up, to trust in God, to believe in themselves, and to ignore all of the world's negativity. To put it in the island patois of my father and his father before him, "stumblin' blocks gatha' no moss."

I learned from an early age that working for yourself is preferable to "the daily grind" of waking up every day depressed, knowing that your effort, your sweat, and your blood will be spent as a small cog in somebody else's wheel, where you will work yourself ragged and someone else will get the credit and the benefit. That was never the life for me. I'm not saying that it's always easy being an independent, self-motivated entrepreneur. It does take stubborn perseverance and the willingness to hold onto your dream in the face of those who say that what you're doing is impossible, a.k.a. faith. There are always going to be people who tell you that you're wrong. They're only right if you listen to them.

I've tried it all, no exaggeration. As you will read, I haven't always succeeded, but I have always given it my all. Clearly, I had a lot to learn, but isn't learning from your mistakes part of what life's all about? This book is about the wisdom I've picked up along my long and sometimes difficult path to success.

I'm stubborn. I'm a hard-worker. I'm an optimist. I'm a true believer. What the hell? I'm Jamaican. I'm supposed to be.

INTRODUCTION FROM BOWEN CRAIG

The tone of this book took a few years to come into its own. Kelly is an adventurous and dedicated entrepreneur, a master chef, and an outstanding story-teller. I just funneled his stories through the prism of an American writer.

We tossed around the idea for writing the book in pure Jamaican patois. We tried out a version of half-"patois" and half-standard American English. Eventually, we both realized that we wanted Americans to be comfortable reading the book for pleasure and not as an intellectual exercise, not having to look up various terms and phrases and "translate" them into American English. That's why we finally settled on the idea of telling Kelly's stories through the prism of my words… and yes, Kelly and I both know that it's all technically the same English language, but try understanding a Highland Scotsman when he's giving you directions. It's damn near impossible, and that's the same language, too. The book is written in American English. Even so, we had to include the appendices with some common Jamaican words and phrases. They're just too cool to not put them in somewhere.

It's all Kelly. I'm just the lucky guy who got to put his life down on paper.

YOU CAN'T START AT THE TOP

Most people don't start at the top, and that's good. Where is there to go from the top but down? Even though I was raised the eldest son of a regionally prominent family, all of that island prince stuff went out the window when I moved to the states. I was just another Jamaican guy trying to make it in America. And I started at the bottom like almost everyone else.

My very first job in the U.S. was at a McDonald's in Washington DC on 13th and K Street. I don't talk about it much because, honestly, I didn't work there very long, but it was my first. I hated it, but name a McDonald's employee who doesn't hate his job? I was still in college. I did what they told me to do. I mopped floors and flipped burgers. I think my fast-food memories only lasted for two or three weeks. Some guy pulled a gun and tried to rob the place, and I quit as soon as he left the building. It wasn't worth dying for a minimum wage paycheck. I'm a firm believer in hard work and its benefits, but ain't nobody gonna take a bullet to protect the golden arches' cash register. As any former McDonald's employee can attest, they don't know how to treat their employees.

My second job didn't last much longer. I worked with my uncle cleaning windows and mopping floors at a DC office building on 14th and G Street. Unlike McDonald's, my boss at the office building never threatened to kill me, at least not directly. A few days into my glorious tenure as a window washer, he did ask me to climb thirty feet on a rickety ladder to clean some windows. Again, I left because I didn't think that wiping bird poop off a window was a cause worth dying for.

I am aware that one of the big lessons of this book is the value of hard work. And I do sincerely believe that to be true. I have faith. A part of me wishes that I could say that it's never worth it to quit any job, but that would just be false. When working conditions are so dangerous that you could die, you'd better make sure that it's something you love. Love is worth dying for. A dream is worth dying for. Ronald McDonald and Grimace are not worth dying for.

EARLY YEARS ON THE FARM

Jamaica has always been associated with certain foods. It's a tropical climate, ideal for yams, coffee, and, our mainstay, sugar cane.

My family had means. They were important people in our little slice of the world. They ran a successful farming operation, knowing that it takes more than just good business sense to get ahead. It takes a warm heart and the ability to love to be able to help others succeed. "Treat people good and good'll come back to you."

They ran a farm in Trelawny, Jamaica, where I was born, in a little town called Rock Spring on August 14th, 1947.

Mother—Amy Codling
Father—Christopher Codling
They're good people. We'll talk about them a little.

Growing up on a farm makes a big difference. It's a totally different childhood from growing up in a city. If my parents weren't working hard in the fields every day, the food would spoil. I started working with them when I was just five years old. It takes so many people, and animals, working together to make the whole thing function. I don't just mean that if you don't work together you, your family and your neighbors starve. The country farms grow the food to feed the people in the cities. So, working on a farm means that you feed an entire country. You learn the value of teamwork. You have to. You either learn that lesson or **everybody** starves.

We had all of the traditional island farm staples. We grew crops: yellow yams, cocoa, many acres of pimenta (also known as "allspice"), other spices including, of course, sugar cane. We had donkeys and mules. Farm animals aren't like the spoiled lap dogs in sweaters you see in American suburbs. Our donkeys and mules worked along with me, my parents, our workers and everybody else.

There's more to the story than just that. My father had around one hundred acres of land, but, a few generations before, my family used to own a plantation. My great-great grandfather had a huge tract of land which, I'm told, was large enough to handle the fifty to sixty people working for him. He used to pay his workers in land instead of money. He would give them a place to live and work and help themselves. He was a determined, hard-working man, but he was also a good and caring man. These were the days before cars and trucks, so he bought a cart and a mule to take the produce to the market. That tradition continued through my parents. Or, to put it another way, in Jamaican patois:

"Mi great-great grandfatha gave away lot of lan' and leave a portion for mi great grandfatha and from him to mi grandfatha, and from him to mi fatha. Motha and fatha take it to a hole new level, with trucks no mules and carts. I work with mi fatha and see what it take."

My father was a brilliant man. He was uneducated. He could neither read nor write, but I remember multiple times throughout my childhood when people would tell me just how smart he was. I distinctly remember once when he'd met with some doctors or lawyers, and afterward one of them told him, "Mr. Codling, if you could read and write, you'd be the prime minister of Jamaica."

If it weren't for my mother, I wouldn't have gotten an education. My father thought that school was for girls and that boys should work in the fields and grow the business. But my mother was stubborn. She kept at my father until he realized that she was right and gave in. So I started in prep school at age three. After prep school came elementary school: first form, second form, third form, then fourth form, and then on to high school. When I was fifteen I was sent to a private Christian school in Montego Bay, Harrison Memorial High, where I studied for four years and was boarded in a private home, at my mother's urging. In the British colonial system, the school is a little different than the American school system. Remember, Jamaica didn't gain independence until 1962. We colonial citizens went from first to fourth form and then took an exam which was sent to Cambridge University to be graded and then sent back. It took from six weeks to eight weeks to get the results back from across the ocean. That's a lifetime when you're a schoolboy. Once you get the results, only then can you even think about heading to college.

My mother encouraged my brothers in their schooling as well. My brother Cleve attended St. Elizabeth High School. My other brother, Eton, the baby of the family, stayed at home and worked the farm. He would send me food and my school clothes every Friday, delivered by some of the market people on our market truck. After finishing high school there was not much for me to do in Jamaica, so my mother sponsored me to come to America.

My two younger brothers, Cleve and Eton, and I were all about two years apart in age. We three all worked the field for our father. As the first child, I always caught hell. If anything went wrong, whether it was actually my fault or not, I was blamed for it. But working the fields was a family bonding experience for us. My brothers, my father, and I were all out there. Sometimes our mother even joined us. Even before I could walk, I remember seeing my parents out in those fields, working hard. That's an early childhood lesson that you don't forget.

I've had to deal with the class system all of my life. I've seen it from all sides. As a young adult in Southern America in the sixties and seventies I saw the racially-based class system. I've lived to see that change somewhat in my life. I worked as a cab driver, earning my way through college, in Washington, DC If anyone can see the class system at work, it's the guy on the other side of the plexi-glass, with the exotic music playing low, carting you down K Street. Now, as a local business owner and entrepreneur, I'm on the other side of the American class system. I've seen this idea since I was a boy.

I used to be a rural Jamaican prince. As the son of a son of a son of a plantation owner, it's no exaggeration to say that I grew up as a prince. That's not to say that I was coddled and kept away from work and the harsher realities of life. I've been working since I was five. But, I was the son of the boss. Everybody around knew it.

All of our helpers as well as my parents made sure that my siblings and I avoided the places where a prince was not supposed to go. There are a lot of places where princes dare not tread. I was not supposed to

9

play with the children of the help. My father, who had a lot of sayings, often repeated the line, "Birds of a feather flock together."

I couldn't even dress like the other kids. Every time I see a young man today with his pants hanging down past his underwear I think of what my father would say. My brothers and I were brought up to respect people and to dress like we expected them to respect us in turn.

I don't want you to think that we didn't have to work. We worked… hard. I had chores to do every morning before I went to school: gathering firewood for the kitchen, feeding and watering the cows, feeding the goats (moving them in between their various feeding grounds and pastures), and making sure that the water drums are filled for the day's work. And all that was before I got dressed and then walked three miles to school. I've always worked and always will. I don't understand the idea of retirement. Sigmund Freud once said that the key to happiness was to work and to love. Well, I do both. It's another island thing. You work, you love, you live.

When I was a kid, if you were messing around and doing something that you weren't supposed to be doing and an adult caught you, you'd get whipped. Other parents felt free to impart discipline on any child they caught doing wrong. Then you'd be faced with the dilemma of telling or not telling your parents. If you tell them, you'd get whipped again, but if you didn't, and they found out on their own, you'd be doubly whipped. I had to face this situation a few times growing up, but, again, like all of the life lessons I learned, I'm glad that I did. Seeing some of the ways that American kids mess around and get in trouble, I'm not sure that we wouldn't benefit from a little island discipline here and now.

My brothers and I grew up on the farm. Our father did operate a store and butcher animals for sale, but primarily he was a farmer. And so, that means that we were, too. We had to make sure that the animals got enough food and water every day. We would cut grass for the animals to eat, who themselves would later be eaten. It's the circle of life and it's a large part of growing up on a farm. We would prepare feed for the pigs and the chickens. Pigs really do eat anything. It's not a myth. Like all farmers, we fed our pigs what was left over, the "crop stuff," reject yams, and whatever we didn't finish from our own plates. Farmers understand saving.

10

Along with my father and our workers, we would also plant and harvest the fruits and vegetables: yams, bananas, and bread fruit. Nobody in America knows what a bread fruit is, but it's common in the Caribbean. They're a green fruit that's just a little bit bigger than a cantaloupe. They grow on trees, really sturdy trees. It takes a strong tree to grow bread fruit. And it takes a savvy farmer to harvest them. They've got to be picked at just the right time. If you pick it too early, it won't ripen correctly. If you wait too long, it will just fall to the ground and probably go bad. It takes two or three months for it to get just right. You've got to pick it right before it would naturally fall off the tree. The ones that we didn't pick in time we'd either eat ourselves, give to the workers to eat, or sell to the workers who were going to the store or the market. If they didn't want it, we'd boil it and feed it to the pigs and chickens. One thing you absolutely learn when you grow up on a farm is to not waste anything, and you learn that lesson fast or you don't survive. Luckily for farmers everywhere, pigs will eat anything. So, even the most disgusting, rotten bread fruit or the yam that you dropped and it split in two or the rotten egg has its use.

Farm life is all about cooking. You cook for yourself and eat your food while you're cooking for your animals. You cook for your animals and they eat their food while you're cooking for your workers. Your workers eat while you're cooking for the store or for the eventual consumers who eat what you sell in your store or what you sell to a middle-man who will sell to a store or a restaurant. We cooked a lot on the farm.

My childhood wasn't all toil and farm life. My brothers and I had our fun. We played. We made go-carts and raced them.

My Father

11

We swam in the rolling rivers, fished, and caught shrimp. We shot birds. We played marbles. We stole meat from our parents' store and cooked it for ourselves (unless we got caught and spanked, it was fun). All in all, it was a pretty good childhood. I have my family and my home to thank for that.

I was fortunate enough to learn the value of entrepreneurialism at an early age. If my father had only farmed I would've learned about running a successful business and how to keep different cogs greased and working as they need to in order to keep the wheel spinning. Farming is a complex life. But my father was an entrepreneur at heart. He looked for ways to expand, and he himself had learned the lesson that it's easier to prosper when everyone around you is also prospering. That's the lesson I took from his truck.

You need trucks on farms. You need them to haul seeds, move farm implements around, and harvest crops. Of course, trucks didn't always exist. In the pre-automotive age, my great-great grandfather had a cart and a mule to bring his produce to market for sale. But by the time my father was running things, the business began to slow down and my parents were losing money on their products. Crops were dying in the fields.

My Mother and my Aunt Cynthia

So, my father saw the simple solution. He bought a truck. It was such an obvious solution in retrospect, but at the time, it was a miracle. He could haul his crops to market when they were ready to sell, not having to rely on a middle man to transport

12

them, and not letting anything he'd grown die in the field. And, of course, father used the truck to help his workers. He'd take his workers' produce into town on the truck too. Remember, my ancestors had long paid their employees in land, which they, then, cultivated for their own profit. So, my father would grab me and we'd help move the food into the city. From the age of ten, I was there with him and the workers on that truck, making sure the weight was right to keep from toppling

My Father

over on those bumpy country roads. One spill and you could lose crops, as well as lives, which are often the same thing when you grow up on a farm. I spent a large portion of my childhood bouncing around in the bed of that old truck.

That truck played a huge part in my childhood. It brought me food and nice clothes when I was in school away from home. It kept my father's business profitable. It kept everyone around my family from starving. It taught me lessons about sharing, making your way in the world, loving your brothers and fellow man, entrepreneurship, and just common sense.

STUFF HAPPENED BEFORE AND RIGHT AFTER I WAS BORN

I hate to admit it, but, according to history, the world didn't just start turning the minute I was born. People had been going about their lives, toiling, loving, building, destroying and doing everything else that people do before I was even a twinkle in my parents' eyes.

Although I can actually remember as far back as when I was only two years old, everything that I learned about my family history before I arrived on the scene was told to me by my mother. I can actually remember my mother being pregnant with my little brother, when I was only two years old. My father came to America in 1943 and stayed for two years, until 1945. At the time there was a program that American companies used to headhunt potential workers from the Caribbean to come to various states and work in different industries in order to help the war effort, and my father was a part of that. Some of his neighbors were sent to places like Florida, Virginia or Pennsylvania to toil in factories or fields. My father was sent to Illinois and worked in a TNT factory. No joke. My dad made dynamite for two years. This was during World War II and so there was a great need for stuff that could blow up other stuff.

Like so many others, it was my father's plan to come to America and work for a few years in order to save enough money to come back home, get married and start a family. He would send his extra money home to his parents to save for him for later. This common storyline is what always seems to get lost whenever U.S. politicians talk about immigration. Most temporary immigrants to America are looking to work hard and save money. This is a good thing for all parties involved -- the people, their home countries, the companies and the politicians from all sides who use them as political footballs. From all I've been told I've put together an image of my dapper father in the states in his crisp, superbly-tailored, three piece suits. It's all very Frank Sinatra/Rat Pack-ish in my head and the pictures of him then tell me that my memory isn't very far off the mark. My dad looked smooth. He had some travel and life experience under his belt. He had a plan and wanted to use his new knowledge and experience to make it happen.

My father's plan was a success, but it was not easy. He truly had to woo my mother. My dad was tenacious. Mother said that she ignored his early attempts to date her, but that dad just did not give up. Although there were other women interested in him, he had his sights set on her. He knew what he wanted and didn't give up on it until he reached his goal. That was just who my father was. He kept on trucking until he got where he wanted to get, even if his destination of choice made a lot of other destinations angry. My dad was, apparently, quite a catch, and so his choice of my mother left a lot of grieving women in its wake.

My father returned home to Jamaica intent on starting a family. He had been sending his parents money from his time in America, expecting it to be the nest egg he would use to start his adult life. But, that was not to be. His parents had spent the money. So, as a compromise, his parents gave him land instead of money. His dad gave him a portion of the Codling family land. That's where he and my mother started their life.

In 1947 my parents had their first child. He was an amazing child, the perfect baby. The Jamaican government considered changing the calendar to make my birthday a national holiday, but my parents were humble people. I was now a part of the world.

Although I was my mother and father's first-born child, I wasn't the first kid born to my father. Unlike 21st century America, Jamaica operated on a much older system with regard to having and supporting children. Rich and powerful men could have as many kids, with as many different women, as they could financially support. They were even expected to. For a poor woman with no hope of social advancement, bearing a child, even one out of wedlock, with a powerful man provided a decent shot at the kid's chance of success in the world. That's how it's been in most societies since we crawled down from the trees. Jamaica in the early and mid 20th century was no exception. Of course, like in other times and places, the children born from a legal marriage have traditionally been given higher roles and more privileges. The wife might not like it and the mother's of the other children almost surely don't like it, but it's worked as a societal model for thousands of years. Maybe it's more natural than what we've got here.

The point is that there were other children on my father's side of the family, technically my half-brothers and half-sisters, around when I was growing up. One half-sister, Monica, was born about the same time as me, maybe just a little before. She was close to the family. I distinctly remember going with Monica and my father, when I was four or five years old, to visit my grandfather, my father's father. He was a happy man, always kind and gentle with us children, enjoying our triumphs and our hi-jinks. He had a head full of thick grey hair and a long beard. He always reminded me of Moses from Exodus, except Moses didn't smoke. Grandpa smoked a pipe. Once, when Monica and I were at his house, he sent us outside to light his pipe from the burning fire in the out-kitchen. Monica must have inherited my grandfather's strong sense of mischief and daring. I remember her lighting and trying to smoke his pipe. Of course, I remember her coughing fit that sounded like she was going to vomit up a lung after she did. She couldn't have been more than five or six at the time. I remember that scene, but what I remember most was my grandfather's face. We had been taking too long, so he crept outside with his well-worn walking stick, pretty sure what we were up to, and watched us from a slight distance. When Monica saw him watching her, she dropped his pipe like it was on fire and ran like hell into the woods.

This fond memory occurred only a few short years before my grandfather passed away. His funeral stands out in my memory, too. I threw a button, a treasured personal item of mine, into the ground to rest with him for eternity.

Growing up in my neighborhood, you either got with the program or you got cut off and you left. There and then all of the propertied men had more than one woman. All the men had wives and, if they could afford it, women and children on the side, too. It wasn't a secret, like a situation like that would be here in America. Everybody knew the deal. The extra families either cooperated with the unspoken rules of the situation or they got cut off and left. That couldn't happen here, the culture is so different. But it is a different country with a different culture and a different set of rules in a different time. Here, if a man gets caught with another woman it's a nearly-instant divorce. Even using the word "caught" is foreign. You couldn't get "caught" doing something that no one thought was wrong.

EARLY CHILDHOOD MEMORIES

Growing up was a blast. I was usually thinking of nothing but trouble. Since I got in trouble a lot, it was probably good that I spent a lot of time thinking about it. I spent the majority of my childhood between home, where I worked with my family, my loving grandmother's house, where I was spoiled rotten, and, for the holidays, in Manchester with my Aunt Emilin, or "Aunt Em," just like in the movie.

Every holiday season I was packed off to Manchester to a little area called Chudleigh. My Aunt Em and my Aunt Caudy hosted us children for the Christmas season. Since I was the oldest nephew and my grandmother's first grandson, I was always spoiled when I was around them. It was kiddie heaven.

But at home, I was always shoved rudely back into reality. As soon as we children were big enough to handle the load, my father put us to work on the farm. My father wanted to teach us how to work our bodies. My mother wanted to teach us to work our minds. And both of my parents wanted to teach us to work our souls. As Seventh Day Adventists, we grew up attending church every Saturday. We attended "Sunday School" before church (even Seventh Day Adventists call it Sunday School, though God only knows why). My mother would always dress us nicely to look like rich and prosperous kids. From sundown on Friday until sunset on Saturday, the Sabbath, we were taught not to work nor play, not to cook nor toil, but to spend time on spiritual matters. Of course, playing is a spiritual matter to a kid, and that's where I got in trouble.

Every year we put out our stocking feet next to our beds in order for Santa Claus to fill them with wonders, toys, candy and magic. When I was around five or six years old, I remembered that everyone said that Santa visited kids by entering their houses through the chimney. Besides being worried about his obvious and inevitable breaking and entering charge, I was also worried for more selfish reasons. WE DIDN'T HAVE A CHIMNEY. This presented real problems for a six-year-old brain to comprehend. I went the Hardy Boy route and set to investigating the problem. I faked sleep, lying in my bed with my eyes held shut, pretending to sleep, but really waiting to see just who or what was leaving me and my brothers presents without sliding down our non-existent chimney. After they believed that we kids were all asleep, I saw my parents sneak in our room and fill our stocking feet with all kinds of toys: cowboy gear, toy guns, firecrackers, and clothes, among other things.

At dawn, my brothers and I ripped into our stashes with the usual Christmas morning kiddie abandon. I felt that, as the oldest, it was my duty to ruin Santa Claus for my little brothers. I told them that there was no Santa. I related to them how I'd seen mom and dad in our room last night, filling our stocking feet with all of these goodies. I told them and then they told our parents. The Jig was up. The next Christmas, I just got money. My parents thought that I was too old for Santa Claus. I realize that I'm kind of the "Grinch Who Stole Christmas" in this story, but little boys are curious creatures by nature. In retrospect, I should have kept my mouth shut and raked in the presents.

GAMES, MONETARY PRIORITIES, AND TROUBLE

At around age six or seven I was doing the things that boys of that age do. We were country kids, so bird hunting was always a recreational option for us. I used to make a homemade sling-shot from the tubes of old truck tires and use that as my weapon. Not to brag, but I was pretty accurate. To this day, I'm confident enough in my sling-shot skills that I'd challenge anyone to a bird hunting/truck tire sling-off. Bring it on.

We also liked to play marbles and tops (or, as we called it in Jamaica, "Gigs"). I was big on marbles. I was good, always winning all of the marbles myself. We also played with tops, which some American kids called "gigs," or at the time "whirligigs." But, there was no toy store, so we had to make our tops. We'd cut hard wood. We'd whittle it down to the right size. We'd tie on the string. The game was to protect your top and let it spin its full, natural spin while your friends tried to knock it over. The spinner usually lost.

As I was getting a little older, I began spending less time with my brothers and more time around boys nearer to my own age. We were all into playing marbles. I was so hooked that I distinctly remember one time defying my mother in order to play marbles.

My mother used to give me money on Saturdays to put into the collection plate at church. I had other uses for the money in mind. Often I would stop before church and spend the money on candy. My church used to have a special plate for orphans, where the donated money would go to children with no parents. Even so, I preferred candy to charity at the time. I clearly wasn't thinking about the lesson telling us that the Lord was always watching us and our actions. When the church elders confronted me and told my parents that I was not contributing money to the poor orphans, I tried to lie my way out of it. When you get caught stealing, you usually lie. It's a vicious cycle. I told my mother that I was being harassed at church and didn't want to go anymore. I thought that she'd let me skip, but she stood her ground and insisted that I go back.

Her harsh words still didn't make me want to go back to church. The next Saturday I again skipped church to play marbles with my friends. I grabbed my stock of marbles and walked to my friend's house where we organized a tournament: Denton and me versus Desmond and Pats. We played all morning, except for a break for lunch where we returned to my house and ate most of the food my mother had prepared for the whole family for later that day (she had to do all of the Saturday cooking before sunset on Friday, so we'd always have lots of pre-prepared food ready on Saturdays). After lunch, we went back to playing marbles. To this day, I still think this next part is really funny.

The tournament of champions was in full swing. The pressure was on. The competition was fierce. I was setting up to make a pivotal shot, lining up my marble when my partner, Denton, told me that my mother was behind me. I tentatively looked around and yes, my mother was there, and she was not happy. She grabbed my tee-shirt by the tail in an attempt to drag me home for punishment. I tried to wriggle free of her grasp. I was trying to spin away and she was trying to spin me toward home. We kept going around and around. My shirt was getting more and more ripped until all that was left was the little collar piece by the neck. I did get away, but trouble was waiting for me when I got home.

I didn't go home for a week.

I hid out at my kind grandmother's house. She continued to spoil me no matter what I had done wrong. I always felt that my grandmother would save me from my mother's wrath. My mom was tough. When she set to beating us, she didn't stop. Here in the States, these days, her particular brand of punishment would lead to a call to the Division of Family and Children Services, but there and then it was normal.

In America they call it "child abuse." In Jamaica we just called it discipline. My mother, like many island mothers, didn't play when it came to beating the hell out of us when we did something wrong. She'd beat us to a frazzle (her expression). My father was a little bit calmer, but more deliberate. If we didn't listen to him, he would call us, hold us while he took off his belt and give us one hit with his belt. Then he'd let us go and give us what we called "a running lick." It was always that way. We knew what was coming to us when we did wrong. And it was sufficiently scary to get us to behave…for the most part. Kids will be kids. Kids will always try and test their boundaries. That's just what children do. But not being able to spank your kids is like denying them breast milk. They're going to grow up without the proper nutrients.

What didn't kill us only made us stronger.

Kids here in America mess up and go to jail. Having a child in jail was and is a family disgrace in Jamaica, so we learned not to do those things that would lead us there. I stayed in near constant trouble in my youth, but, thinking back, it was mainly minor disobedience. We didn't steal cars. We didn't break into people's houses or snatch women's pocketbooks. That's real trouble. We just did what boys do. It comes in many names: mischief, hi-jinks, fooling around, and some other, less family-friendly, terms.

THE LITTLE LADY WHO TAUGHT ME HOW TO COOK

I owe a lot to my grandmother. She was the one who spoiled me. Her house was where I ran away from home when my parents were mad at me, usually for a good reason. This tiny woman set an example for me of how to live a life overflowing with kindness, love and happiness. She always had a smile on her face. I can still picture her with her long flowing hair, the large glasses she began to wear later in life and a cigar or pipe in hand, cooking for her six kids (three boys and three girls). Nobody believes me when I tell them, but she used to smoke cigars by putting the lit end into her mouth and inhaling. I swear it's true. I don't know how she managed not to ever burn her mouth, but that's what she did. She was her own woman in a time when that wasn't as easy as it is today. She taught me how to pray. She taught me how to love.

Among all of the lessons my grandmother taught me, I'm probably most grateful for one — she taught me how to cook.

My grandmother didn't believe in measuring. To her the idea of a measuring cup of salt or a teaspoon of brown sugar seemed absurd. She was the master of the "dash." She'd throw a dash of allspice or cumin into the pot of whatever she was cooking. Then she'd taste test it to see if she'd added enough. That was her system. It worked. I do the same thing myself.

"Mama," My Grandmother

25

She'd use this system even with the famous Scotch Bonnet pepper. This over-the-top hot pepper is a staple of Jamaican cooking. It puts the Texan peppers and the Mexican peppers to shame. Its sweet and spicy taste is uniquely Jamaican. It's hotter than most of its competitors, but it doesn't leave the lingering aftertaste that burns your mouth and temporarily deadens your taste buds, like so many of the other peppers. Just dipping a Scotch Bonnet into a pot of boiling water gives it enough spice to taste. That's how hot it is.

My grandmother would cut up the Scotch Bonnet real fine, chop up some onions and add a dash of water. She'd drape Ackee or saltfish with her special sauce, or add it to squash or cabbage. I still use her technique for some of my best-loved menu items.

We had "Out Kitchens" in Jamaica. These were outdoor pits where we'd slow-roast pig, chicken or another animal. Out kitchens were traditionally all natural. They were made of wood and leaves, with a natural arbor, strong enough with the wood to withstand wind and the elements, but delicate enough with the pimenta leaves which lined the wood to trap the heat and the smell of the smoked meat inside. We'd line the leaves, usually pimenta (allspice) leaves, with pig intestines and lay them on the top of the arbor after they had been cooked in order to continue infusing them with the heat from the burning fire and trap the aroma in to give them the signature island taste. Since I try and honor my ancestors as much as possible, and because their way was better than most modern conveniences, I have an Out Kitchen in every restaurant I open.

If you're a Southern American and over a certain age, you've eaten pig intestines. You probably know them as "chitlins." They go by many names and are loved by people all over the world, but it's best not to think too much about what they really are.

My grandmother loved to cook pig intestines. I used to watch her clean the insides of the pig. She'd literally turn them inside out to clean out the waste leftovers, since that's what intestines do in the body, even in pigs. Then she'd lay the clean tubes on the top of the out kitchen's top layer of leaves. Then they'd smoke. Then they'd smoke some more. After that they'd keep on smoking. My grandmother would smoke them for a month or more before they were ready to eat. A month! They called that "well-cured" meat. In this day of instant gratification and microwave frozen meals, can you even imagine preparing a meal a month in advance? It's just not done now. But it used to be. And it was delicious.

I remember once, when I was little, I argued with my mother (I was a rebellious kid, so we wound up arguing a lot.). As any good mother would, she taught me "not to eat from other people." It's the Jamaican patois form of the American expression "don't take candy from strangers." It's a good lesson, but I loved my grandmother's food and so I argued with my mother, telling her that I should be allowed to eat from my grandmother. I went straight to my grandmother's house and told her what her daughter had said. She said to tell my mother that I could eat from her. My mother relented and agreed, smiling. She adjusted her saying to "don't eat from other people... except your grandmother."

My grandmother was a deeply religious woman. She prayed daily. She wasn't sanctimonious or holier-than-thou, but her faith was a big part of her life. She believed in miracles. After a miracle happened to her, I did too.

Much later, I was living in Texas, struggling, but managing, when I got a phone call from my mother telling me that her mother was sick in bed. I bought some diet soda and other sugarless treats for her, packed two sets of clothes and hopped the next plane home. When I got there, my little grandmother was indeed in bed and sickly. I said, "Mama, I'm home." I always called her Mama. I saw that she was having problems with her back and was squirming, so I turned her over and saw multiple bed sores. Having worked in the medical field in DC, I knew what to do. I told my uncle, who was her caregiver, not to give her any more sugar. Although most of the family had given up on her, I didn't. She'd never given up on me, so I wanted to return the favor. With some difficulty, I helped her up and out of bed. With my arm around her frail body, I helped her outside for the first time in weeks. She started to pray for me. Even when she was sick, she was still thinking first of others and praying for ME. I had to get back to Texas to work and my family and so I did. I called my mother again a few months later and she told me that Mama was up and walking back and forth to church. "No way!?" So, I hopped another plane back home to see it for myself. I was racking up some frequent flier miles seeing my beloved grandmother through her illness. When I got to Jamaica, I caught her walking back home from church. My mother hadn't been exaggerating. Bed-ridden just days before, there my grandmother was, walking miles on those hard, country dirt roads. Seeing me, she took my hand and we danced in the street. It was one of the most beautiful, most miraculous, most poignant and important memories of my life.

UNCLE DEZ

My uncle Desmond, or "Uncle Dez" as we all called him, was a mentor, a friend and a brother all rolled into one. He was only a few years older than I, so we bonded like brothers, but he was also a hard-working, knowledgeable man, so I learned a lot from him. He was born in 1945, and I came along just two years later. We grew up together, learned about life together, and got in trouble together. We used to party together all the time. We'd go to the local dances. That's what the young people did for fun then and there. It was such beautiful innocence.

When, due to my mother's insistence, I left the family home and ventured to Montego Bay for school, Dez was the one who convinced me that it was for the best. I was scared. Although it seems like such a small distance looking back now from the perspective of a world traveler, back then it was a long way away from home for a farm boy to venture. I'd never even considered traveling that far away, but that's where the best school around was located, and my mother would accept nothing less than the best for her first-born son. It did not take me long to make new friends at school, but at first I was frightened in the way that all young men leaving the womb are, and I missed my Uncle Dez every day. Every vacation and school stoppage meant that I could go back home for a bit, back to the farm. So, I did. And when I did I worked with, shared my thoughts and dreams with, and partied with Dez. As much as anything Dez was the very embodiment of home in my mind.

During the occasional school breaks, I'd sign on with Dez's construction crew to make a little pocket money. I was his assistant, learning the trade from a master. I'd follow him around, slightly puppy-doggish, but let's call it more like an apprentice. I'd watch him work. I'd carry his tools. I'd make runs to the store to replenish his materials so that he could keep working to finish whatever individual job he had at the time.

I also did something that I always did without, of course, knowing that it would become my career many years later in a totally different country. I cooked lunch for Uncle Dez and his workers. Using the skills

29

taught to me by my grandmother, his mother, I would cook Jamaican food and feed a crew of hungry workers each day I had on school break. It felt good, but I still had no idea that cooking would become anything more than a hobby for me.

Uncle Dez built houses. He taught me about construction. He taught me how to "flash cement" so it's nice and smooth when you lay it down. We didn't have the fancy tools I later worked with in the states, like the "Popcorn Machines," paint sprayers and nice paint brushes. We did it by hand like the builders of Medieval Europe and Ancient Egypt. We smoothed out the mortar with pavers and trowels.

Uncle Dez took me to school when I first began in elementary school. He also taught me how to talk to girls and what to look for in a girl. That's a valuable lesson for a young man and one that I've put to use many times. He was funny as the dickens.

Uncle Dez was a unique and amazing person. He was a man of God who believed in doing for others and he fervently trusted that if you put God first in everything you do, you can achieve greatness in any area of life. Not just anyone can do it, but my beloved uncle managed to infuse the Lord in his work building the houses and shopping centers that he was contracted to build.

When I started writing this book, I knew that I wanted to, needed to, honor my Uncle Dez. But, I didn't realize just how big a part of my life Dez inspired. His work had taken him to a few different places, and he'd tell me exotic stories about far-away lands like Canada and Belize. It was Dez who inspired me to travel. When my mother, after she'd been in America for a while, sent for me, I used Dez as my lifeline to home. I'd write him every month and tell him about the differences between Jamaica and America, how the roads are bigger in the States, how the people speak so many different languages, and how even those who speak our language do it in such a weird and different way. I told him how nobody prepared home-cooked meals in America, and that there were so many different restaurants to buy chicken, beef, sandwiches, whatever you wanted. And, stranger still, I told him how there are so many different little rules here, and how most of them make no sense. One of my first days in the U.S. a policeman saw me urinating into some bushes on the side of a road. He stopped and told me that I couldn't just pee wherever I wanted. I had no idea. In Jamaica, if you've got to go, you go, no matter how many motorists might see you. It's no big deal. After the policeman told me the deal, I started to walk away and crossed the road. He told me that I couldn't do that either, that I was "Jay-walking." What? Jay-walking? Americans don't cross streets? He said that there were certain designated places where people are supposed to cross streets, magical places called crosswalks. I adjusted. I still think that there are too many rules and they make life harder, not easier, but you adjust to whatever situation life throws at you.

Whenever I got the chance, I'd come home and see Uncle Dez. We'd talk. We'd party. We'd enjoy home-cooked food. And we'd cross streets with reckless abandon, at any place we wanted. We'd pee anywhere we pleased. When you've got to go, you've got to go. The very idea that urinating is somehow indecent is crazy. The policeman who told me what was what said that if I did it again I'd be cited for what he called "Indecent Exposure." Dez and I would laugh about that one a lot. How can something that every single person does every single day possibly be indecent? It's crazy.

SCHOOL DAYS — PART ONE

1950s

When I first started elementary school, my uncle Desmond used to take me to school every day. There are some similarities to school all over the world, but there are certainly some differences, too. We did have a cafeteria for kids who wanted the cooks to prepare their lunches, but most of us went home for lunch. It was common. We had to be back at school before one PM.

School started at nine AM sharp. They locked the doors at exactly nine. Oh, they'd let us in if we were late, but that turning of the key came with a belt snapping from the teacher.

My main point is that in school, much like in Jamaican society at large, kids were not spoiled. American kids are spoiled rotten. I know that it's not politically correct these days, but kids today could use a good belt smacking.

We worked from an early age and, like the discipline, it didn't hurt us. Again, you couldn't get away with that here and now. When I was just a wee baby, I remember learning about that work ethic. I'd watch, wrapped in my baby blanket, as my mother joined my father working in the sugar cane fields each morning. My mother was a hell of a woman. My uncle, Desmond, her brother, saw my mother working in the fields one day and I remember his saying, "Sissy Girl, you not a woman, you're a womanie." That was a compliment. It meant that she was more than a woman. She was powerful, hard-working and possessed of a spirit which would never allow her to give up. She and my father did something that few ever do. They built a dynasty. They created something that lots of people lived off of, something that provided work, food, love and opportunity for much of the surrounding area.

I've said it before, but my mother was the backbone of the family. She knew how to get men to work. She'd always feed them before coaxing them into the field. She'd feed them hearty breakfasts of green ba-

33

nana, yellow yams, dumplings, ackee & codfish, eggs, and maybe some calaloo, an island vegetable which is reasonably close to turnip greens. She'd prepare meals that would "stick to their ribs," as they say.

That's why I always wanted to come home from school for lunch. My mother was a damn good cook. She'd cook for all of the men working with my father in the fields. I'd eat and then head back to school. After school I usually didn't go directly back home. Often I'd stop by the river and go for a swim with friends. And when I did eventually return home, my mother would always want to know why it took so long. She knew how much time it took to walk home from school. I could've lied to her, so there was no point in that. She was going to find out the truth one way or another anyway. That's the thing. Someone was always watching. Someone was going to tell her what we did, so lying was usually just delaying the inevitable. Some other mother would call her and tell her that she saw her boy down at the river. This usually happened before we got home, so she already knew where we were, and we knew that she knew. When I got home, she was there with the belt ready. My friends' mothers all did the same, too. Here they call it "child abuse." There we called it "child rearing." We called it "community." We called it "life." And we were better off for it.

Sometimes we kids were included in some of the adult fun. Occasionally my father and his friends would invite us boys to go bird hunting with them. Those were great days and they followed a pattern. Mother would cook lunch for the men and me and have it ready before we left in the morning, early in the morning. We'd have to get up at 4 AM. We'd pack into two cars and head for the woods where we'd stay all day. The trick to a successful bird hunt is getting into the woods and settled before the birds begin to feed. Getting a bead on them right before they'd drop their guards a little as they'd begin to feed in the early mornings is the key to shooting birds. We'd need to find their feeding trees and areas where the "slug seeds," or big seeds, were that the birds craved, and know which birds liked which slugs. Wild cherry seeds and wild grape seeds were always popular. Parrots like orange seeds and pimenta spice seeds. We'd hunt for king pigeon (a really big pigeon, much larger than American city pigeons who beg for bread crumbs in big cities), parrots, doves, partridges, and bald plates (a super-fast bird with super hearing skills, very difficult to bag, named because it has a white spot on the top of its head that looks like a plate). Hunting these birds requires patience, rising early in the morning, and knowing what they like to eat. Bald plates eat "slug seeds." Sometimes we'd hunt for wild hogs, but they were rare. Mainly we were bird baggers.

Going on the hunt with your father is a male coming-of-age ritual as old as the cavemen. It's a skill that is passed down from father to son everywhere, in every country, in every time, all over the world. There's not a lot of big game (buck deer, grizzly bear, moose) in the islands, but think about it. It takes much more skill to shoot a lightning-fast, hyper-alert bird with the ability to fly than it does to nab a five hundred pound grizzly bear. Anybody with enough bullets can take down a deer. It takes a real island, prepared, seasoned hunter to nab a parrot. I'm only half-kidding.

SCHOOL DAYS — PART TWO — SECONDARY SCHOOL

1960s

    You call it high school in America, but in the rest of the once-British, still vaguely colonial world it's called secondary school. Since my mother was Seventh Day Adventist, when I was the appropriate age, I was sent to the religious secondary school in Montego Bay, Harrison Memorial School. I was fifteen. It was the first time I'd ever been away from home for any length of time. Montego Bay is one of the bigger cities in Jamaica and, for a country boy like me, raised among loving fam-

ily in a familiar environment with rules that I knew and understood, it was a difficult adjustment. Montego Bay, or Mo Bay, is the capitol of St. James Parish, a big city and a tourist destination. It was unlike anything this country boy had seen. The cars sped by on the streets of the city, kicking up dust and loose gravel. In the country, you can hear the trucks rumbling from miles away and if you're walking, you can always bum a ride. It wasn't like that in the city. The pace of life was faster. The smells and sounds were

Me

different. They were everywhere. There were all kinds of people from different places in the world, mainly other Caribbean islands, but not exclusively. Montego Bay, as you probably know, is a coastal port city. Port cities are international by their nature. It was all new to me, both scary and exciting, full of possibilities I'd never even dreamed of and full of just as many new fears.

My mother "boarded me out," meaning that I lived with a family in Montego Bay. It's common in the islands for secondary schoolers to live with families in houses near the school. That way, the mothers of the kids feels like there's at least some parental supervision. Mister and Misses Brown, the people who boarded me, had two sons of their own who were roughly my age: Vincent and Bobbise. We all attended the same school, Harrison Memorial.

I lived those years as a second-class citizen, like a medieval squire to Mr. and Mrs. Brown's two knighted sons. Luckily, thanks to my parents and my grandmother, I knew how to cook, how to clean, how to wash

Me

clothes, and how to sew on a sewing machine. Thanks to those skills, I was given a slightly higher position in the hierarchy of the Brown house, but not much higher.

We got into trouble, as kids always do, but compared to the kind of trouble kids get into today, it seems so innocent that it hardly seems like I should use the same word for it. We didn't rob people or carry guns. Our trouble was more like mischief. We'd climb onto the flat, one-story rooftops of the multi-colored Montego Bay neighborhood houses and jump from roof to roof. It was such a rush. It felt like flying, except when it didn't. One time my friend fell into a yard with five barking dogs. We thought that he would get caught by the dog, but once he landed, caught his breath and shook the stars out of his vision, he realized that the dogs weren't eating him alive. They were all chained.

I may have been a rebel, but I like to think that God was still looking out for me. He kept me out of all kinds of other trouble, too. The Brown kids and I would pick the neighbor's mangoes (which is technically stealing, but snagging fruit seems worlds apart from ripping people off at gun-point) and delight in the forbidden sweetness of this island delicacy. We'd sneak into the movies when we were supposed to be studying. We didn't have girlfriends. We had to make our own fun. And we did.

There was a park behind the Brown's house. We'd play there during the week. On the weekends there was always live music at a club on the other side of the park. The Brown kids and I would tell their parents that we were going downtown and then we'd sneak over to the club. Because we attended Seventh Day Adventist school, we weren't supposed to go to places like that, but we were sixteen and seventeen-years old, so we did it anyway. On school nights, the curfew was 8 PM. On weekends, it was 9 PM. Predictably, I pushed that envelope often. I tried to get away with as much mischief as humanly possible.

Since my mother was in the States, making money, she would send me nice clothes and a little bit of pocket money, and I took advantage of that to make friends with everybody, boys, girls, seniors, juniors, everybody. Even when I was in secondary school, I had nice stuff. Kids are attracted to shiny things everywhere in the world. So, my mother, inadvertently, helped me become a popular kid. She also helped my social standing in another way (again, one that she couldn't have predicted). I was ALWAYS the cook, the one who made my friends wait and let their stomachs rumble while I cooked up some saltfish in hot sauce or prepared some Jerk chicken or fish in a quickly-assembled out-kitchen. We'd have picnics on the beach and I'd always do the cooking. My friends ate better than most kids anywhere, any time.

Harrison Memorial School is where I met the first love of my life, Carol Lawson. You never forget the first time you fall in love. It's burned in your memory for life. Along with being smart and beautiful, Carol was a stubborn girl, rebuffing my continued advances. I was new to the idea of dating, so I tried anything to get close to her. Every time I tried to talk to her she'd ignore me. I used to follow her after school as she walked to her father's office just to talk to her. Perseverance is one of the keys to success. That's true in business and in love. I kept on trying to get pretty Carol to notice me and finally she did. The first time she spoke to me was to tell me that she was about to move 70 miles away to go to West Indies College, the Seventh Day Adventist college, in Mandeville in the Parish of Manchester. I had a cousin who was attending West Indies College, and I asked her if she knew Carol. She did. I stayed in touch with my first love through her. After I graduated CAP Secondary School, I came straight to see her at college, and

My Daughter, Trecia, at 12

spent some time in the country before leaving the island for America. Since my mother had arranged for my visa, I joined her in Washington, DC, where she had been living for some time, but I never forgot about my first love, Carol Lawson. We stayed in touch. My parents even sponsored her U.S. visa. We got married when she came to the states a few years later. I told you that I was persistent.

Carol gave me my only daughter. I will be forever thankful for that.

MY AMERICAN JOURNEY—PART ONE

1960s-70s

My American journey began when I came to the United States in October of 1969. However, my mother's had started some time before. When I was still in school in Jamaica, mother had received a telegram from a family in America asking her to come and work for them, taking care of their children, as what is called a "nanny." I had never seen either of my parents work FOR anyone other than themselves. We'd always had people working for us, not the other way around. As I was later to learn, life takes many twists and turns, and you've got to learn to roll with the punches, as they say.

My mother wasn't a soft and cushy woman. She was and is loving, but she also has always understood life's lessons and, like any good parent, wanted to impart them to her children.

As soon as I'd touched down in Baltimore, Maryland, and saw my mother in this foreign land for the first time, she wasted no time in telling me what's what. No smothering with airport kisses and presents and cliché phrases. She looked me dead in the eye and told me that she'd brought me here to make something of myself.

In patois, or to make the word "patois" into patois, you've got to say "patwa":

"Mi bring yo ya to betta yo self. If ya get in a troble don call me if yo sel drug or steal and go a jail doen call mi, yo fatha and mi na sel wi lan to bail ya."

Her bluntness shocked me at the time. I hadn't even officially set foot on U.S. soil yet, and here she was, lecturing me about what I shouldn't do before I'd even cleared customs. Of course I didn't know then how many, let's just say, uninformed Americans thought that all Jamaicans were weed dealers, and that my mother was simply warning me and teaching me right from wrong in her own way. These days I call my mother every night to tell her how I am and to thank her for making me the man I am today.

I came to the States first under a student visa. I went to college in DC.

Coming from Jamaica to the United States was a big, big change for me. These Americans were doing everything the wrong way. Dear God, they were even driving on the wrong side of the street. Were they crazy or what?

I couldn't even understand what people were saying at first…and we were technically speaking THE SAME LANGUAGE. But I listened. I read people's lips. I paid attention to the nuances of speech patterns.

The first thing I did in this new country was to travel to downtown Washington, DC to buy a few things for my mother at a huge G Street department store, Murphy's. Remember, this was 1969 in America's capitol, not the most peaceful time to be in that particular city. Bobby Kennedy and Martin Luther King had been assassinated the year before. There had been riots in DC. And here I was, happily walking down a giant street in a strange land, barely understanding the language, going to a humongous department store to shop for my mother. It was interesting.

Once I returned to my mother, she, once again, informed me that I was on my own here in America. I had to find my own way around town, around this new country, around life.

So, I did.

I started attending Cortez Peters Business College in 1969 in DC at 14th and K Street, right in the heart of the city. I received my associate's degree in Business in 1972. After finishing at Peters, I briefly attended Strayer Business College but did not wind up finishing there. While I was going to Strayer, I worked my way through school by driving a taxi and working at a hospital to pay the school tuition and buy books.

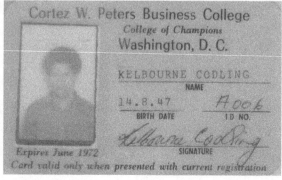

Cortez W. Peters Business College
College of Champions
Washington, D. C.

KELBOURNE CODLING
NAME

14.8.47
BIRTH DATE

A006
ID NO.

Expires June 1972
SIGNATURE

Card valid only when presented with current registration

42

MY AMERICAN JOURNEY — PART TWO

1970s

After coming to the States at the age of 21, I realized just how much of an adjustment life was going to be for me. Everything was different than in Jamaica. There was no one to wash my clothes for me in America. There was no one to cook for me. There was no one to wash the dishes after I'd eaten. There was no one to clean the apartment for me. Just what was a Jamaican prince to do?

Luckily, unlike others from similar backgrounds in this situation, **I was prepared.** My mother had taught me self-reliance from an early age. She'd insisted to my father that her children be educated properly and completely. And she did it for just this very reason. Also, she was willing to lead me through the changes like a tour guide at a college or a museum.

She took me to the downtown supermarket and showed me how to buy, what to buy, and then what to do with it once I'd bought it. In my own words, she weaned me as if I were a calf or a kid (a baby goat, because, in many ways, I was still a human kid, despite extensive education and some practical work experience from an early age). To put it simply, I was shown the ropes by my own mother…and it took.

I now started to see life as a broader picture, a panorama of shades, themes, ideas, and possibilities. After finishing Cortez Peters Business School and receiving a degree in Business Administration, I attended two other colleges, Montgomery Community College and Strayer Business School. I took some classes and soaked up the economic, business knowledge like a sponge. I didn't finish at either of those colleges, but, unlike a few of my classmates, I did learn and take to heart what they were trying to teach.

I'd been working on my father's farm since I was a wee lad. I knew how to work, and thank God for that lesson, since I had to work to be able to afford school here. While attending classes, I did various things

43

to pay the bills aside from being a taxi driver. I worked in a Jewish nursing home. I worked at a suburban hospital in Maryland. I even worked at McDonald's and a few other fast-food restaurants.

Remember, this was not the most racially tolerant time to be a black man in America. I experienced racism first-hand, in ways that black kids today wouldn't even think could possibly have been true. And it wasn't all that long ago. I was spit on. I was kicked in the chest. I was cursed. I can't even count how many times I was called "a damn nigger." Heck, I was called almost every racial slur you can think of. But, even though this line of thought was unfamiliar to me, I took it all in stride and didn't let these expressions of abject hatred and pure ignorance make me feel like anything less than who I was and could be (the Jamaican ethos is all about love and togetherness). That kind of ignorance reflects much more of the one doing the evil than on his target. I told myself that those people were old, set in their silly ways, and didn't know any better. Many of the residents of the nursing home were merely old and losing their minds.

Despite tolerating this abuse, one day even I had had enough, so I quit the nursing home job and went to work at a furniture store in Rockville, Maryland. It was called Levitz Furniture. I worked there for four or five years. It was a decent working environment, or at least better than some of my previous ones.

Like with all of my previous jobs, I learned the lessons of entrepreneurship while I was at Levitz. Even a bad job can teach you a thing or two if you're willing to learn. I had to load and unload furniture from delivery trucks. This meant that I needed to know where the various types of couches, beds and chairs went in the store…and why. Bassett chairs needed to go to this area. Pulaski couches were supposed to be displayed in that area. The proprietors had done their homework and knew how to create an enjoyable shopping experience for their customers that would both facilitate an easy shopping jaunt for their buyers AND be able to maximize their own profits. Once again, I took note.

That being said, loading and unloading furniture is hard work. Ask anyone who has ever tried to do it. So, one day I saw a very good friend, and we started talking about the job at Levitz and how hard it was. I was the ONLY one doing the heavy lifting. I'd already learned the lessons. My friend said that he could get me a job at the Washington Hilton hotel as a desk clerk. He said that he'd put in a good word for me. So I went to the Hilton, had an interview and got the job.

My job at the Hilton was to check in guests, take them to their rooms, and ensure that they were satisfied with all that their rooms had to offer. I also had to check the unfilled rooms to make sure that they were vacant, to make sure that they were both available and satisfactory for check-in for new guests. Sometimes the system wasn't as quickly updated as it could have been, so the clerks like myself, had to check each room in person before we checked in new guests. Nobody wants to go to their hotel room and see someone sleeping in their bed, or eating their porridge. There's a reason the Three Bears fairy tale has survived these long years. Again, as always, I was making mental notes. Hilton is a well run business. They're successful, and there's a reason for that success. I knew that I wanted more than just being a hotel desk clerk some day, so I was paying attention to what worked and what didn't at every stop along my journey.

In 1972, my high school girlfriend, Carol, came to the States for school. She also attended Montgomery College, where she too, studied Business. I worked at the Hilton for about five years and, during that time, I got married to my high school girlfriend. It was a beautiful wedding. We had a child, our only child, Trecia.

I had a gold 1972 Grand Prix SJ. Man, that was a sweet ride. It had brown leather interior, real leather with that distinctive smell of freedom and possibility.

Even in marriage, especially in marriage, there are lessons to learn. We were young. We were foolish. We had an active social life...too active. We had a lot of friends and, like so many other young people, we had jumped into marriage too soon and partied waaayy tooo much. Just trying to live life in the American way, trying to have it all, and have it all right now, put too much strain on our marriage. It wasn't the most original reason that a marriage didn't last, but I did learn a thing or two. I learned that I should've paid more attention to family life, to my family, to raising my child, the way that my parents had with me. I was trying to live the American Dream....and I had forgotten all of the things my parents had spent years teaching me.

I lost everything.
I lost it all.
I lost my job, my wife, my cat, everything.
I was back at square one.

MY AMERICAN JOURNEY—PART THREE
PARTYING IN THE NATION'S CAPITOL/FAMILY MATTERS/CABS AND HORSES AND MONEY...oh my.

So, I was still living in Washington, DC. My life had just fallen completely apart, but, as always, I took it in stride and "rolled with the punches," as they say. One of life's biggest lessons, and one that sometimes takes years to fully learn, is that everyone falls, everyone fails. It's as inevitable as the sun and the rain. But, it's how you are able to pick yourself back up that matters. So, I did that.

Things were very different in DC. For one thing, it was so much more expensive than what I was used to. Money became an issue. I needed it. I didn't have it. So, I found ways to make it.

I know that these prices sound paltry nowadays, but moving to a city where gas was 42 cents a gallon, a telephone call in a phone booth was 10 cents, and cigarettes cost 35 cents a pack struck me as ridiculously expensive. I may not have had much money at the time, but I did have ideas and I had family. My brother had come to the States. My mother did live-in work, so she would go to work early on Monday morning and my brother and I wouldn't see her again until Saturday. So this meant that my brother and I were left to our own devices for a majority of the week. Another overused American expression applies here — "When the cat's away, the mice will play." And we played.

We had so many parties that I can't remember them all. We made sure that everyone had a good time. There was no violence, nobody shooting guns, and few fights. It was just a bunch of young people having fun. Knowing that we could turn even partying into a slight money-making opportunity, we charged people $2 to get in the door. This covered our expenses and everyone had fun. It was the 1970s and my Afro, my bell-bottoms and my well-heeled shoes (we called them James Brown shoes) were the uniform of choice for the men of the time. Remember, I'd just gotten divorced and was, once again, for the first time in a while, a single man on the prowl. There were ladies everywhere. My brother and I enjoyed the 70's to the fullest extent.

Honestly, there's so much that I could talk about that happened at that time in DC that it would take an additional book to fit it all in. Instead, I'm going to write about two important pieces of my history in that time and place: gambling and taxi driving.

I'm a very good gambler. I loved playing the ponies when I was living in Washington, DC. And I could pick winners. I wasn't an obsessive, nuts-and-bolts, addicted gambler who knew the minute details of the rearing of every horse, the statistics of every jockey and the exact weather conditions of the track. Though I did glance at those factors, basically I was more of a gambler-by-feel. I looked for coincidences, names that jumped off the page at me, signs from the horse lords that pointed me toward winning picks.

There are a lot of tracks in the mid-Atlantic region. I was close to Bowie, Pemlico and a few others. I used to get up early on Saturday and drive down to the track in time to place a bet on the first race…if I wanted. But usually I waited. You see, that's a part of the key to successful betting. I didn't bet on every race. I didn't feel the need to. I picked one of two horses in whatever race I felt like and then waited patiently for my race to start.

I was so good that oftentimes the obsessive gamblers, the guys who spent their every waking hour at the track and bet on every race, basing their emotions on whether their picks won, placed, showed, or lost, would would ask me for my picks for the day. Those guys didn't always take my advice, but, when they did, they usually won. I'm not saying that I'm Rain Man. I'm not Miss Cleo. But, I know that God doesn't know the meaning of the word "coincidence." Let me tell you a story about one particularly memorable day at the track. It's a good story about family secrets, gambling, money, lies, mild betrayal, and the unassailable wisdom of motherhood:

One Saturday I wanted to go to the track, but I didn't have any money. So, I asked my mother if I could borrow just a little money. She said no, like I figured that she would. But, soon she left the house. Now, I knew that what I was about to do was wrong, but I did it anyway.

My mother had one of those precious leather-bound Bibles with the zippers that went all the way around and held it together. That's where she kept her spare cash. I knew this. I was raised with her Christian values and I knew that it was wrong, but I waited until she had left the house, snuck silently into her room, stealthily unzipped the Bible and stole twenty dollars from inside her precious Bible before leaving for a day at the track.

I picked up my brother. I spent five dollars on gas, a hot dog and a soda and bought a program for 50 cents. I was going to bet ten to twelve dollars and hold back a little just in case. I didn't bet the first race. I didn't bet the second race. But while the ponies were finishing up the second race I read the program. There they were. In race number three, I saw two clear signs. One of the horses was named **"Foolish Pleasure"** and another was named **"Here Comes Mama."** It was fate. If those weren't signs, then I don't know what is. I had to bet those two. One of them had 60-1 odds to win and the other had 70-1. I put down $6 for wins and $4 each for placing and showing (in horse speak those stand for coming in second and third place, respectively). I tried to tell my brother and my friends to bet on those two with me, but they didn't listen. I tried to tell some of the professional gamblers who asked me for advice, but they just laughed at me and bet the favorites. I was always one to pick long shots and then hedge my bets by picking them to win, place AND show, meaning that if my horse finished in any of the top three positions, I'd make money.

Out of the gate, "Here Comes Mama" took the lead immediately, followed quickly by "Foolish Pleasure." Although they were both long shots, they both jumped out in front, followed closely by the horse which was actually favored to win. Around the second lap, my two picks were still in the lead. Kicking up mud, wheezing with exertion, my two fated long shots sped around the oval track, ahead of the pack, their jockeys bent low to avoid wind resistance, hitting them with their crops and praying to the pony gods for luck. They rounded the track and entered the third lap, with my two picks and the favorite still battling it out for supremacy, all three of them leaving the rest of the pack in their wake. Finally, they came to the finish…aaaaaannnnnndddd…it was "Here Comes Mama" by a nose. I won. I won.

49

Actually no matter which of the three had come in first, I was set. Being a savvy better I knew to cover my bases with small bets that would, if I won, pay off big. And boy did they pay off that day. I left the track with almost $4000. I was giving my brother cash, buying drinks and lunch for everyone, and giving out twenty dollar bills like they were tissues.

When I got home I snuck back into my mother's room, quietly, like a tiger on sand, unzipped her Bible and put $20 of my winnings back in to replace the money I had stolen. Later, when my mother returned home, I was still flush with pride and victory. I said her, "Mother, how would you like it if I gave you some money?" She looked me right in the eye and asked knowingly, "Did you steal twenty dollars from my Bible?" Mothers always know.

I drove a taxi in Washington, DC. It was a crazy job, especially for a relatively new immigrant in a large, sometimes confusing, metropolitan city full of all kinds of people from all over the world. I did this for over two years.

Driving a cab in DC wasn't exactly the safest job in the world. I had co-workers who got robbed, often. They'd get a call for a pick-up from the airport and the next thing they knew, they'd have a guy pointing a gun in their face, demanding all of their money. But, after awhile you develop a bit of a sixth sense for the routes. You knew if a call from the dispatcher sounded fishy, and you didn't take that call. After a bit I got in good with the dispatchers. I was kind to them and brought them sodas and snacks and they gave me good pick-ups. It's that old golden rule. The dispatchers would give me the cushy airport fares, sometimes taking people from Baltimore to Dulles International Airport, or even the rides from the airport to the NIH (National Institute of Health—where they experimented on human "guinea pigs"). I distinctly remember picking up one guy from the airport one day and dropping him at the NIH building. He was a nice looking man with a full head of hair, a healthy complexion and a happy attitude. Later I went back and picked him up from the NIH building and took him back to the airport. He didn't look good at all, sickly and pale. About a month later I went back to pick him up from the NIH to take him to the airport once again. This time he looked awful. He was as pale as a ghost. He had lost all of his hair. I asked him what was wrong, and he said that they were doing some kind of experiments on him. That was the day that I asked my boss to put up a shield between the driver's seat and the back passenger seat, which they did.

The taxi company was also a front for a mobile drug dealing unit. I didn't know that at first, and, once I did, I just kept my head down and let other people do what they did, while I just did my work and kept my mouth shut. People used to sell drugs to customers as they were taking them from one place to another. In order to make it easier, the dispatchers were in on it. One day they got busted by an undercover cop posing as a passenger in search of drugs. When I got back to the office, I saw all of these police cars and my fellow cabbies face down on the ground in handcuffs. What a day that was! It shocked a lot of people. I was shocked when I saw who was dealing. This Jamaican cabbie was one of the only drivers who DIDN'T deal. How's that for breaking stereotypes? A lot of people I thought would've been clean, weren't. The allure of all of that money can tempt any man.

And those are just a few of the stories from my time in Washington, DC. There just isn't enough paper and ink in the world to write all of the DC stories.

WE USED TO "DO IT UP RIGHT"

Ahh, I miss the 1970s

I'm remembering fondly my time in Washington, DC. I was young, free, full of hope and energy and love and enjoying every minute of every day in this new country. I was working, taking classes at Montgomery Community College and Strayer Business School and partying. Oh yeah, I used to party. But, unlike today, back in the seventies we "did it up right."

I love thinking about those days at Pemlico, or Malcolm X Park, or the Amphitheater. Those were good times. A friend of mine opened one of the first reggae clubs in DC. Those American girls went crazy for our positive, inclusive music with a beat you can "get down to." That's how we used to talk.

Washington has a reputation for violence these days. That may be true now, but it wasn't when I lived there. We never had to worry about people pulling guns in the middle of a house party. We weren't there to fight. We were there to eat, drink, meet girls, dance and have fun. I'm not saying that everything was rosy, that there weren't occasional fights. If two guys were going to fight, they'd take it outside. Everyone made sure that they went out and settled their differences outside of the party zone.

Young men fight sometimes. That's been true since the days of the cavemen. When someone threw a punch at me, you better believe I

This guy looks a little like me

53

threw one back. But, you see, that's the difference. We punched. We fought with our fists. Once in a while someone would pull a knife, but that was rare and it was frowned upon. Now everyone has a gun. Guns are like cheating. Shooting someone isn't a contest. It isn't even a real fight. It's just stupid.

EVERYTHING REALLY IS BIGGER THERE:
MY TIME IN THE LONE STAR STATE
Texas part one

1970s-80s

Texas is different. It just is. My experience in the Lone Star State was almost the opposite of what I had seen and done in Washington, DC. Texans delight in saying that "Everything's bigger in Texas," and there's some truth to that. It's big. There's a lot of land, a lot of empty space, a lot of humongous belt buckles, huge hats, large cowboy boots, giant trucks and large people with large egos. Everyone there also thinks that they are bigger than everyone else, that their state is somehow the center of the known universe. If that's true, then our universe is centered around some huge assholes.

I saw the stereotypes that people associate with Texas first-hand. There really are a sizeable number of rednecks driving pick-up trucks with gun racks and places to load their dead deer carcasses. And they really did have massive prejudice against Blacks, Jews, Chinese, and Mexicans. I had no idea what I was getting into.

My brother had asked me to join him in Texas. I was curious. I was looking for the next chapter in my own story, so I took him up on his offer and traveled south. I learned quite a bit about entrepreneurship, general business practice and just plain human psychology. It wasn't always pretty, but sometimes the roughest times are the times when you can most easily learn something useful.

I first got a job in a large department store in Beckford, a little town on the outskirts of Dallas/Fort Worth. It was a Sears, easily one of the most recognizable names in retail and one of the pioneering department stores whose catalogs have become a memorable part of our collective past. Everyone has heard of Sears. Anyone over a certain age can remember their famous catalog. I've even heard stories of people using the catalogue pages as makeshift toilet paper during lean times.

I was placed in the toy department. I only stayed in that department for a brief period. I do vividly remember one little girl who asked to feel my hair and, after I consented, touched my hair and marveled that it was soft and fluffy. I could've taken this as coming from a bad place, but it was just a child's curiosity and wonder. I just smiled. That's a business and life lesson which has stuck with me. A smile goes a long way. It makes customers happy. It makes you happy. It works.

Being a good salesman, after one particularly busy Christmas rush period, the manager asked me to stay on at Sears, and I agreed. They moved me to the paint department. There I learned how to mix paint, create all of the different shades and match colors. I worked there for one year, walking to and from work every day, and seeing my (then) current situation, I could've gotten depressed. I could've thought about all that I'd lost from my time in Washington. I just kept on saying to myself that yes, I had messed up, but that simply meant that I had to work things out. So, that's what I did.

One day at the Sears store I saw a car for sale, and so, I bought a car. It cost $450, a decent amount for me then and there, though I dare you to find a working car that only costs $450 today.

Then my work situation improved. I was working at Sears. I worked hard. People saw this. One day a woman came in the paint department, saw me working and asked me if I'd ever considered working for one of the big paint stores in the area. It turns out that she worked for Kelly Moore Paints, at their factory store which manufactured all of the paint for every Kelly Moore store in Texas. They shipped to Dallas, Houston, Austin, all over the large state. After filling out an application, I talked to the General Manager and was hired that very day. He took me down to the paint store and introduced me to all of my new co-workers. I was the only black employee at Kelly Moore Paints at the time, but they were pretty accepting, at least for Texans.

I worked for Kelly Moore Paints for two years. At first they sent me all over: to Garland, Irwin, Plano and Dallas. I was using most of my paycheck to pay for gas. After talking to the GM, he agreed to bring me closer to where I was living, meaning that I was working back at the factory store where I'd applied in the first place. This turned out to be another blessing and another learning opportunity.

The factory store was by far the biggest and busiest of all of their stores, and I had to quickly adjust to my new environment. We had to know the paints by their number, what type of paint it was (water-based, stain, etc.). When I first arrived there they demoted me to the stock room, most likely because I was, once again, the only black person in the store. As had happened so many times before, I could've taken this as the insult that it was and quit, but, again, I looked for the opportunity in this new situation. I got to be very good at my job. I got to know the customers by name and figured out what they were going to buy. I was fast. I was so fast that they called me, "Lightning." When I saw a customer driving up I quickly filled out the paperwork and before they had finished their coffee I had loaded their paint and presented them with their paperwork, so they were ready to go. Lighting is fast and powerful.

The inside salespeople worked me hard, stocking the store and the warehouse. Again, I didn't mind. I put my head down and worked hard. Eventually my boss presented me with a chance for advancement. The final decision was between me and another stock room worker. I got the job over him, which made him angry and he promptly quit. At that point I was working both as a salesman and in the stock room. While many of my co-workers would take every opportunity to slack off, drink coffee and smoke cigarettes, I just kept on working hard.

Eventually, I had had enough of working for other people, and working toward my dream but not yet being there. So, I left and started my own painting company. We'll get to that in a bit.

LESSONS LEARNED — I had learned to work hard from my father. He had a decidedly different style than I did, but he always stressed the value of hard work. He was a hard man in his way, but he was smart and able to adjust. I remember, Dad wouldn't fire people, but man he would yell at them. If he saw a worker lying down on the job, he'd scream, "Get your @##@$ back to work!" I remember telling him, "Pop, if you wouldn't yell at people so much they might work harder." He'd reply, "If I don't curse them, they curse me." He had a system, but I wanted to test his ideas. One day when Dad was away I remember seeing all of the workers lazing around in the shade, avoiding work. I could've yelled like my father, but instead I tried logic. I said to them, "If my dad was here you couldn't be slacking off like this." They thought about it for a minute and saw where I was going. "Mr. Kelly, you're right." They went back to work and worked hard that day. When my father returned he asked me what I'd done to get them to work so hard. "I talked to them, Pop. I didn't curse." Dad shook his head and finally said, "I guess I've been doing it the wrong way all this time."

A lot of people are lazy. But, despite what some people think about the laid-back island culture, an idea that is used to sell American and European vacation packages to paradise, there is an undercurrent of hard work to the island culture. I remember when I first learned about food stamps and unemployment benefits. When I was laid off from Levitz Furniture Store in Washington, a co-worker told me that I should go and apply for food stamps. "What are food stamps? Is that like unemployment?" I asked. He said that it was. I told him that Jamaicans don't believe in unemployment. I told him that unemployment meant finding another job. It's just how I was raised.

Hard work is a necessity. It's a given. But you also have to have a plan and the ability to think ahead. I like to have fun, but I've always looked to what I can accomplish next, where I can spend a little money in order to make more down the road.

STILL ADDING COLOR TO THE WORLD:
Texas part two

After I'd worked at the paint store for more than two years, one day there was a shake-up (bad paint pun intended). The General Manager strolled in one day and fired the Store Manager, the Assistant Manager and some of the staff, leaving just a few employees and myself. I started doing everything, taking on more responsibility and learning how to run a business. I was ordering the stock, going to the bank to make deposits, and keeping everything in order. This lasted for about six months. I was basically running the place. And so, I asked the General Manager if I could be promoted to the Assistant Manager job, seeing as I was essentially doing it already. Although other employees and even some of the customers had told him that I should have the position, he didn't see it that way. So, I gave him my two weeks' notice. I remember that he told me then, somewhat angrily, that I could quit right then and there, but I stayed for the standard two weeks. That's the way it works.

On my final day I turned in my key, gave over my alarm system password, walked out the door and didn't look back. I was now on my own. It was time to stop working for other people and start fulfilling my dream.

It takes money to start something new. I asked my mother for a loan to get started, but she refused due to some of that all-too-common intra-family rivalry nonsense. My brother had warned her not to loan me any money, telling her that I would use the money on foolishness. And, seeing as I had once stolen from her Bible to gamble on the ponies, even though I'd won big that day, I understood. These things are going to happen, especially when family is involved. You can't let them get you down.

I consider myself a religious man. Even though I don't attend any regular church service, I've always believed in God, the Creator, whatever you want to call it. As I was starting my first business, I got down on my knees and asked Him for help, for guidance. I asked Him to be my foundation and make me strong enough to accomplish what needed to be done.

With the Lord's strength propelling me forward, I did what I'd always done. I worked hard. I had saved what little money I could, after having to pay out daily living expenses from my time at Kelly Moore. Of course, I had to actually buy the equipment before I could start my own painting business. You must have the proper tools for the trade to get any job done. I bought a drop cloth, rollers, brushes, paint, tarps and other necessary painting accessories.

I started my first business in much the same way that most people do. There was a lot of shoe leather worn out on my way to independence. As a means of introducing myself to potential customers, I had some business cards printed. I put up fliers. I stapled cards to fliers and went door-to-door handing them out, letting people know that I had the equipment and the experience to get the job done.

I talked to all of the local contractors and builders, trying to get my foot in the door. Needless to say, it was not easy at first. I had a few cards stacked against me. I was new. I was black. I was a foreigner. But I was also determined.

I would bid on every job that came available, furiously scanning the local paper to find new job sites. Knowing that I needed some help, I teamed up with a partner, an experienced painter and a bit of a hippie, Randy. Although we were putting our blood, sweat and tears into finding business every day, it was, like I've said, a huge challenge at first. In fact, we were about to give up when one day, seemingly out of the blue, we got a call from a builder who told us that he had some houses and apartments which needed painting. We went immediately out and bid on the job. Two weeks later, the builder called and told us that we had won the bid. It was a good day.

Hard work builds on itself. Getting the first job was great, but then you have to do it and do it well. I worked hard, just like I'd always done. That one job turned into two. Those two turned into four, then five, then six. You get the idea.

EVERYTHING'S BIGGER IN TEXAS, EVEN THE ASSHOLES
Texas part three

I'd been out on my own for a little bit now. I was running a successful painting business with a partner. We had the tools, the will and plenty of jobs. I was finally out from under the constant burden of working for somebody else. Things seemed to be going smoothly... but I was still in Texas.

A racial Texas incident that has stayed with me happened in a Fort Worth country bar. It was named, I swear to God, Billy Bob's. There's some redemption in this story, more so than in the one which follows. Setting the scene, it's the 80's. My brother and I are dressed to the nines, in three-piece suits, out for a night on the town. Unfortunately for us, that town was Fort Worth, Texas. One of the guys on my work crew, a white guy, invited my brother and I out for the night. We should have gone to a more friendly place, but my brother and I were proud. We felt that we should be allowed anywhere and, even in that time and place, we strutted our stuff and, on many levels, tried to push the envelope. When we three walked in we were immediately accosted by (surprise, surprise) a drunken, racist, redneck telling us that we didn't belong at Billy Bob's. He was pressing his point. You can feel it in the air when a situation is about to turn violent. This one was on the verge of that. His and our volume levels were starting to rise and, though I can only speak for myself, I was about to throw a punch. The owner (I'm not sure if he was Billy Bob -- that's a pretty common name in Texas) stepped in and ended it. With two bouncers in tow, he rushed the drunk redneck. The two huge bouncers grabbed him from either side and they proceeded to literally toss him out the door. It was a scene from an old Western movie. The owner felt bad that we had to deal with that. He apparently hadn't realized that any two black guys in Texas have to put up with racism every day, all day, but the owner meant well. He offered us free drinks all night. We'd have accepted, but that would've defeated the purpose. We didn't want to be treated differently than anyone else, positively or negatively.

I've got a lot of "I can't believe this is really happening to me" awful Texas stories, but there's one that stands out as the worst. When you read it, you'll know why.

We had earned a big job painting an entire complex. We were tasked with painting in a nice subdivision. Like most start-ups companies, we'd started small. We painted one house and did a good job which led to two and so on. This was an important step for us. The way we looked at it, this was our first major job.

One day we were on the job and another painter, a white guy I'd never seen before, drove up to us. Being polite and friendly people we said "hello." He told us that we didn't need to be working here, that he did all of the painting here, in effect that this was "his territory." It sounded a little Old West, but it WAS Texas. I could've told him where he could stick it, but instead, being naturally inclined toward getting along with people, I tried diplomacy. I pointed out that we had landed the job legitimately and that there was more than enough work to go around. That's not true. I said, "I'll go anywhere and paint anything. I don't see your name painted on this subdivision." He was an ass and had made me angry. He left and I went on with work, not thinking anything about it.

Then, a few nights later, I was at home, unwinding from a long day, when I heard a girl's scream outside my house. Looking out, I saw a frightened, naked girl covered in blood. I opened my door to help her. As I did, she approached me and reached out to touch me with her bloody hands. At that moment, something inside of me snapped, and I had an inkling of what was going on. I backed up. Using a stern tone, I told her not to touch me, to sit down on the curb and wait while I called the police. I went inside and got her a towel to cover herself. She was shaking. Something about the event felt wrong, a little off. "Trust your intuition." It's a valuable lesson to learn.

When the police arrived I was once again fortunate that there was a black EMT among those who answered my call. After the police did their jobs and took our statements, the black EMT pulled me aside. He told me that if he hadn't been among those who had showed up, I would most likely already be in handcuffs. He said that I was a lucky man. I was a lucky man. I am a lucky man. I'm not sure that it doesn't have more to do with mental attitude than luck, but I don't know.

I had a neighbor who worked at the courthouse. She later told me what I had suspected since the night of the incident. My painting competition had set the whole thing up to get me out of the way. Being the only black contract painter in the area, I was used to a few dirty looks and more than a few rednecks using racial slurs, but this was something entirely different. That painter and some of his friends had set the whole thing up! I soon came to a painful and terrible realization. They paid the girl to let them beat her. That's just sickening.

I did see the man, the evil mastermind, a while later. I could've hit him or blessed him out, but, instead, I simply told him that he should be ashamed of himself. Apparently he was since he didn't say anything and just lowered his head and walked away. Texas?!

I hear that even Texas has gotten better on the racial front, but I don't think that I'll believe it until I see it.

Sure, that was the most extreme example of exactly why we should all forget the Alamo, but there were certainly others. The mentality in Texas was, when I was there, still very Old West. Fighting was just a part of the culture, the scene. I even got into a fight with my first business partner, Randy Poe. He and some of the guys who worked for us were always after me to go out to what they called "tittie joints" with them after work. I always asked them what that meant and they laughed. Eventually they explained what it was. I love women as much as the next guy, but I just didn't think that that was my scene. One day I gave in and went with them. It was my first Texas tittie bar experience.

I should explain Randy a bit. He was a fascinating guy. Randy was a direct descendent of the famous macabre poet and author, Edgar Allen Poe (that kind of lineage casts a long and strange shadow). Randy was a hippie. And Randy had some mental issues. He was a true artist with paint. He could've done anything. But Randy let his mental problems and the opinions of others dominate his everyday life. We were good friends, but people were always telling Randy that he shouldn't be playing second fiddle to a black man. It was Texas.

I sympathized with Randy's situation. He had a lot of people telling him that he could do better than he was at the time. Coming from a prestigious family like he did can be both a blessing and a curse. It's not easy living up to greatness. Since my father was a successful man in his own right, if I'd stayed in Jamaica I probably would've had similar thoughts. I liked Randy. I always told him, "Don't listen to what other people say. Be better than that."

I've always trusted my intuition. It's gotten me through many rough patches in life. I should've trusted that little voice inside that night, too. After a night of lots of booze and lots of sexually frustrated men staring at what's just beyond their reach, my partner and I got into a fight outside of the club. I don't even remember what it was about. We were pretty drunk and acting stupid. He was irrationally mad. He punched me. I caught his fist and stopped him. I held him tight to keep him from fighting. He was young and thought that he could take me, but I've always been pretty scrappy. Imagine it. Think of the scene: me, with my huge Afro and era-appropriate heeled James Brown shoes, wide lapelled collared shirt—him with his hippie rags and long pony tail, fighting outside of the Texas tittie bar. The cops came and asked me if I wanted to press charges, but I didn't. The next day he apologized, but the anger and resentment lingered. Three weeks later he quit and we split our equipment down the middle. We had $15,000 and I gave him half. I still had one truck, one paint sprayer, and half of our rollers and brushes.

A few years later Randy died under mysterious circumstances, which, though tragic, does seem appropriate for a relative of Edgar Allen Poe's. He was found one day with the back of his head blown off and a shotgun lying on the ground in the woods in an apparent suicide. Something didn't add up. The position of his body was off. He was discovered leaning forward with the shotgun in his hands. Shotguns are powerful and knock the shooter back when they fire. If Randy had actually shot himself, his body would've been blown backward by the force of the recoil. Like his famed ancestor, Randy was pretty heavily into drugs, so I suspected foul play.

We had been close friends. I remember, when we first partnered up we made a deal that if anything happened to either of us that the remaining guy would take care of the dead guy's wife and family. That's one of those vows you only make with good friends. And all of it ended one horrible drunken night outside of a Texas tittie joint.

64

EASTBOUND AND UP

1990s

The changing fortunes of the housing market is one of the biggest and most important economic indicators (gauges) we use in our society. It makes sense when you think about how many different industries are dependent on building new houses and remodeling old ones. As a painter, I got to see this first-hand.

After the bottom fell out of the housing market, in the 1990s, things began to get very tough for me. Construction companies were folding all around me. This meant that there was little or no new building, which, of course, meant that there was much less work for those of us who painted the houses. In Texas at the time worried homeowners were selling their houses for a fraction of their worth. It got so bad that eventually everyone was feeling the crunch.

One day a friend of mine called me and asked if I wanted some work in Fairfax, Virginia. Knowing that I was a good painter and a responsible businessman (as well as my, then, current situation), he thought of me when he was offered a larger job than he could handle on his own. After thinking about it for a few days, I packed all of my gear and headed east. We had 350 apartments to paint. This job saved me.

Once again, life threw me a curve ball. Life's like that sometimes. Learning how to "roll with the punches" is one of the most important lessons anyone can learn in life. I was thinking that everything was going well for me. I had a good wife and family in Texas. I had plenty of work in Virginia. I was traveling home every two weeks to check on my family. The sun was shining. The birds were chirping. It seemed like my life was on track. But, it wasn't. Sometimes we all think that people are with us when they really aren't. While I was working hard to get the apartments ready for lease in Virginia, a friend from Texas called me and asked me to come home and look after my things. I was confused. My wife was supposed to be taking care of the family affairs back home

65

in the Lone Star State. My friend told me that she'd moved out, taken our daughter with her and cleaned me out, taking all of "our" stuff with her.

I caught the next flight back to Texas. My friend was right.

I was sad, of course, terribly, unexpectedly sad. I had thought that the two of us were going to spend the rest of our lives together. But, instead of wallowing in what could have been, I did what I've always done when things go bad. I moved on. This time I moved to Virginia. I called my landlord, gave up the house and settled where the work was. I started all over again…again.

Life is going to present you with situations like this. Even the most successful people have had to deal with tragedy and unexpected changes at some point. It's how you deal with this inevitability that defines you as a person.

That's not to say that I wasn't incredibly disappointed. Back at work I had a hard time getting my misfortune out of my head. But, like the song says, "Starting all over again/It's going to be rough/But I can make it." I just kept on trucking.

ANOTHER LESSON LEARNED — It's in the darkest moments that we discover who we are. In these times we often think about earlier events that, when they happened, seemed trivial and insignificant. Back when I was painting in Texas I had a job painting a woman's house. We grew close and talked often about a variety of things. Not to brag, but I did a great job on her house, leaving no mess, no paint drippings. When I'd finished the job, she turned to me and said, "One day you are going to be a very famous person." I just laughed. She responded, "You laugh now, but one day you will remember what I told you." She was right. Thirty years later, I can vividly remember her words.

MORE ROUGH TIMES AND A LITTLE REDEMPTION

After the initial job in Fairfax, Virginia, there was nothing else for me to do. My friend went back to Texas to stay. I still had contacts and friends in the nation's capitol, so I decided to stay around the area. I had all of the equipment. I had all of the know-how. I could paint anywhere. An old friend told me to contact Cross Builders. He even called them and set up an interview for me with the owner of the company. After talking to the owner I was contracted to paint my first house for them. So, starting over once again, I got a crew together and worked tirelessly on that first house.

Cross Builders liked what they saw in me so I was given more and more work. I even painted the owner's personal house. Things seemed to be going reasonably well, given the circumstances.

I'm a trusting person. I like to give everyone a chance. But, sadly, not everyone should be trusted. Some old acquaintances, people I thought were friends, from my old days in DC were working with me painting for Cross. I didn't know that they were crooks. I just remembered the good old days, 10-15 years ago when I first lived around the area. But I had been romanticizing the past. These two "friends" went behind my back and tried to steal both my equipment and my jobs. One day they tried to steal all of my equipment. They

Younger Brother and Mother

67

even talked to builders behind my back, attempting to secure my jobs for themselves. They tried to rip me off, plain and simple. It took the builder we were contracted with to tell me what was happening. When I confronted them with the evidence of their betrayal, we got into a fight and had a falling out. Then, they went their way and I went mine.

I was pretty well totally alone at this point. I was back at the familiar "bottom of the ladder." These things are going to happen to anyone in life, and I feel like I've been at the bottom of that ladder more than my fair share of times. But, like always, I just got up, brushed my ass off and went right back on climbing.

Even with my positive attitude, this period was a rough one, for a long time. Bidding on painting jobs in DC was becoming more and more competitive. There were a lot of paint outfits and some of them had been around for long enough and were well-organized enough that they could underbid me. I simply wasn't getting enough work to justify continuing to do what I was doing.

I did what a lot of people do at their lowest points. I called my mother. She was, at this point, living in Florida. Like any good mother, she was always worrying about me. It's just what mothers do. One day, when I was nearing that familiar bottom rung of the ladder, she called me and told me that there was an extra room in her house available for me if I needed a

Mother and Younger Brother

change in scenery. I did. That's how I moved to Florida.

In Florida, I was once again faced with that same decision, that one that seems, at times, to be following me around like a shadow. I could give up or dust myself off and keep going, stronger than before. And, once again, I chose the latter. I went job hunting, mostly for positions in the con-

68

struction field: painting, refinishing furniture or drywall, hanging wallpaper, anything. I was having no luck. This lasted for quite a while. Finally, a friend hooked me up with a general

Me

contractor. The contractor had been told that I was the kind of worker who would stay until the job was done and that I could be trusted. This sounded good. The man asked me to come in for an interview. I was upbeat. But when I got there, the boss, the owner of this company said that he could pay me five dollars an hour. I was speechless. He said, and I quote, "This is the sunshine state."

I'd been doing this for years, had run my own outfit, had been the boss myself and I was being offered the salary of a high school dropout. I didn't lose my cool…but I didn't take the job either. I just got in my car and calmly drove away.

This entire period was difficult. I was living in my mother's extra room. I was taking odd jobs wherever I could find them, doing a bit of painting, a bit of wallpaper hanging, a little drywall, whatever I could find. And, Lord knows, I was trying to stay positive. I'm a positive person, but tough times can wear on anybody.

Strangely enough, I was saved by a hurricane. It sounds weird, maybe even a little mean-spirited, but life is a funny thing sometimes. Hurricane Andrew roared into Florida, destroying homes, businesses, families, people's lives. But it wasn't all bad if you were in the construction business. I really don't mean to sound callous, but it was the utter devastation wreaked by this horrific natural disaster that saved me. I traveled south and, along with hundreds of others in my line of work, followed the trail of destruction and found more work than I could handle. Using all of my skills, I got steady work and got myself back on my feet. One job led to another, to another and so on. People's insurance checks went toward re-building their lives, their homes, their shops, and, through them, my own life as well. I even spent some of the money to buy a little booth and stock it with new equipment: spray guns, clamps, etc.

Life involves a lot of change. To succeed, you must be able to roll with the changes life inevitably throws at you. The insurance money began to run out and my formerly steady stream of work began to slow down. Much like when I was in Texas, I had to start thinking about what to do next.

Things were about to change…again.

ON THE ROAD AGAIN

I was in Florida, the state that proudly calls itself, "The Sunshine State," but all I could see were dark clouds. I felt like everything had fallen apart on me...again. I was living with my mother. I was still working with furniture, occasionally picking up a painting job or two and selling fish on the weekends. In what little spare time I had, I went to the track. I guess I've always been a gambler. But, like any decent gambling man, I had a plan. I've almost always had a plan. Those were some dark days for me. My business and my marriage had fallen apart. I'd been betrayed by the people closest to me. There's a difference between the sad, hopeless gambling addicts, trying desperately to pick a long-shot winner out of the pack, and the man who gambles intelligently, picking his battles, hedging his bets, and only betting big when he's pretty sure that he's picked a winner. Years of gaming have taught me that it's better to be in the second category.

I'm not saying that I've always won. If you're going to gamble, sometimes you're going to win and sometimes you're going to lose, just like in life. It's only during the low times, like those Florida days, that I was actually counting on gambling to make money. I wish that I could say that I had a "moment of revelation," some grand lesson from God, that told me to change my ways. It would've made for a better story. But, I just got tired of it. I got bored of struggling to make ends meet. And so, once again, I changed direction in life.

I was still determined to work for myself. I was still resolute in my desire to achieve that American dream. I just needed a new plan.

One day, while selling my fish in Florida, I was talking to a friend, a fellow Jamaican ex-pat. We were discussing my circumstances. I told him how competitive the market was becoming and he suggested that I should try selling fish in Georgia. There's fresh fish available everywhere in Florida. It's a peninsula. Anyone with a rod, a bucket and a street stand can hawk fresh fish in Florida. That's not true in other states. I didn't know anyone in Georgia, so my friend hooked me up with his

71

nephew in Atlanta. I called him and he told me to come up and check out the scene. There were a number of Jamaican restaurants around the area, all of which were constantly in the market for fresh-caught fish. The plan came together in my mind. I called another friend in Miami and told him about my plan. He was going to go into business with me, but backed out at the last second. Even so, the plan was solid.

It may not look like it on the map, but it's a long drive from South Florida to Atlanta, Georgia. I generally averaged twelve to thirteen hours per trip. The first time, I had no idea that it would take me that long. I can remember that first time, after having driven for more than half of a day, coming into Macon, Georgia and seeing that Atlanta was still 80 miles away. Man, that seemed like an eternity.

When I arrived in Atlanta, I called my friend's nephew and he met me off of Interstate 20, at Wesley Chapel Road. Immediately after arriving at his place, I tossed my suitcase down and we hit the road, searching for potential restaurants to sell my fish. I scoured the greater Atlanta area, looking for customers in Decatur, Stone Mountain, and other suburbs, as well as in the city. He led me around the city, and I met the owners of restaurants, letting them know that I'd be back regularly with fish "fresh from the sea." The Dekalb Farmers Market was a beautiful sight. They sold every food you could think of. Customers who were looking for fruit, meat and vegetables straight from the field shopped at places like that. But, when we got to the fish area, all of their fish looked rancid and old. The fish smelled like it had been sitting in the hot sun for three weeks, and some of it had. Seeing this was the clincher for me. I knew that there was a market for fresh fish in this inland city. So, I did what I always did when presented with a new life challenge. I put my head down and went to work. People always say that hard work never killed anyone. My father said that, too. He was right. He also taught me to stick to a plan. When you make up your mind to do something, you can't let anyone or anything stop you.

After returning to Florida, I went about setting up. I rented a van from Enterprise. I bought large coolers to pack with ice to store the fish. I bought fresh snapper, king fish, salmon, and flounder, among other creatures of the sea. I planned my route from the Florida Keys to the capitol of the South, Atlanta. If car rental agencies had offered frequent

72

driver miles at the time, I'd have earned a free trip to Pluto, I drove so much.

Being the only person selling fresh fish in the area, I had the market locked. My customer base grew and grew. People began to associate me with fresh fish. I slept in my van during the week. Yes, it did smell a little like fish, but, unlike old fish, fresh fish smells pretty good. And, at the time, that fishy smell was the odor of success. I kept a bucket of water in the van and a scaling knife to clean the fish. Most of my customers were ladies who didn't have time to clean the fish before they cooked them. I would clean them so thoroughly that all the ladies had to do was wash them and cook them.

After about a month of selling fish from the back of the van, I was looking around for a more permanent storefront. I saw a little place for rent inside of a Jamaican store. I met and and got in good with the owner. I started buying other things for him in Florida and transporting them up to Atlanta, things he couldn't find in Georgia. We did very well for a time. My fresh fish drew more people to his store. In fact, I was doing so well that he got jealous. I began to notice that when I'd leave for a delivery to a restaurant, by the time I got back to my van some of my fish had swum away. Some of my money swam away, too. Be careful who you go into business with. Some people simply cannot be trusted. My friend, whose business I had helped grow, was stealing from me.

THAT LITTLE VOICE INSIDE SAVES ME ONCE AGAIN

I've made a habit of listening to that inner voice, that little internal warning system that some call intuition, others call God, and still others call common sense. That little guy has saved my ass numerous times. That time in Texas when I was being set up with the bloody woman was one of the most striking examples of this voice saving me from doom, but it wasn't the only one.

I'm generally a trusting soul. I like to give everyone a chance. Even after being burned by so many untrustworthy people in the past, I've managed to maintain a sense of optimism and a belief in some degree of goodness in my fellow man. But, I've been burned...a lot.

When I was still delivering fresh fish from Miami to Atlanta, I was starting to get back on my feet, but I still needed to make some extra money. I was doing pretty well and beginning to establish myself as the hard-working Jamaican guy with the good seafood. People associate my island with delicious fish direct from the ocean, but it's not the only thing people think of when they think of Jamaica. People think of bright, vivid island colors. They think of sandy beaches and ancient pirates. But, they also think of herb. A lot of people, when you mention Jamaica, immediately think of ganja. So, my friend in Atlanta asked me to smuggle ten pounds of weed up from Miami to Atlanta on one of my fish runs. I could stash it between the produce I was also bringing with my fish. When he asked, I agreed, not thinking of the possible consequences, other than making some much needed money. I could use the money to buy a van instead of being forced to rent. I could even buy a stand, a place of my own, to sell my fish.

I was all set to go, but the night before I was set to leave and make the run, I heard that little voice, that familiar warning, telling me that something felt wrong about the scenario. Something was off, and someone was reminding me of that.

The plan was for my friend in Miami, who was an upholsterer, to make some pillows and sew the herb inside of them. It was a decent plan, but the night before I was about to leave, the voice in my head showed me a vision of myself getting caught. It told me that if I were to get in trouble, it couldn't help me. I bolted upright in bed, sweating and thinking, "This cannot be happening to me." So, I didn't let it happen. The next morning I called my friend in Miami and cancelled the order.

Even so, I still had a job to do, so I drove to the market and picked up my fish and produce. I hit I-75 and headed north. I remember stopping at the Waffle House and eating some eggs, grits and toast. With a calm mind and a full belly, I continued north. At the Florida/Georgia line I passed under a bridge. There was a GA state trooper waiting, idling under the bridge. After I passed the bridge, I saw that he pulled out and began following the car directly behind me. Keeping my eyes on him, feeling that same feeling of premonition, I knew that he was gunning for me. The trooper did eventually pull ahead of the car behind me and took up a position trailing me. And, predictably, after a bit he turned on his lights. I pulled over, thanking God repeatedly for His warning.

The trooper called me <u>by my name</u>…before he had even asked to see my driver's license. That was a pretty big and obvious red flag. I did give him my license. He asked me if he could search the van and I told him that he could, with pleasure. I was feeling pretty smug. I knew what was happening. He didn't. He went through all of my belongings and rifled through my produce. Finally, he asked me if I had anything illegal in my coolers. I told him, "no." He reminded me that if he found anything illegal in there that he could lock me up. I told him that he could empty the coolers, but once he did, he would destroy my seafood stock. And then he began to do just that, which, since it was directly hurting my business, made me pretty mad. I was fuming and threatening to sue him, the State of Georgia, everybody. I had 700 pounds of fish in there that needed to stay on ice to stay edible. The trooper realized that there was nothing illegal in my van, so, turning to me, he asked me how many miles it was to Atlanta. It was around 250 miles. He said, simply, "Have a nice day."

Driving the 250 miles, I was thanking God the whole way. When I did arrive in Atlanta at the store where I was set to deliver my goods, they were all surprised to see me. They had expected me to have a new temporary residence, one with bars on the doors and group showers. The whole thing had been a set up to get me out of the way to make way for one of my so-called friends to take over the fish delivery business. Since his was the shop where I had been selling my fish, I had to relocate and find other restaurants and markets.

HOTLANTA

1990s-2000s

I have so much to say that, at times, I do not know where to start or where to stop. I guess I'll stop when I'm dead. Not before. I'm not a believer in idleness or retirement. I could write an entire book on my experiences in Atlanta alone, all of the trials, the tribulations, the joy, the pain, the betrayal. It might make for decent reading.

I've mentioned in previous chapters my various partners in the past and how most of them did me wrong. When I started out in Atlanta I was entirely on my own. I had delivered fresh fish straight from the seas of Florida to all of the Jamaican restaurants in Atlanta for years before I moved there. So, I knew the scene. I knew what it lacked and what it had in abundance. I knew where I could fit in.

I was selling fish from a friend's garage until I discovered a run-down trailer on Covington Highway, near Panola Road, way out in the country. It was pretty far out there. There were no houses for a mile around in any direction. It was all woodland and trees as far as the eye could see. Still, it was a better location than my friend's garage. People associate freshness with the outdoors. It makes sense. Nobody wants to think, even subconsciously, that the fish somehow came from a garage.

I debated starting my business in a location that far off the beaten path. Georgia had been good to me, and I desperately wanted to relocate here, but it took a lot of thought before I decided to take the leap and open up a fish stand that far away from any potential customers. But, I wanted to do it, and so I did.

I only sold fish for about two years. I already had a few loyal customers who knew that my fish was fresher than the competitions, but, after a few years the fish business began to get very competitive. So, I did what any successful businessman will tell you is the only way to operate in a situation like this, and I branched out. I began cooking some traditional Jamaican dishes like Jerk Chicken, Oxtail, Escovitch

Fish and Jerk Pork. The word started to get out and things began to pick up a little. As with any business, word-of-mouth is the best advertising. And soon the word got out around Atlanta that if you wanted to get the best fresh fish and Jamaican food around, you had to drive out into the country a bit, to my place. I soon found a different location a little closer to civilization.

It was a dump, but I knew that I could fix it up. A friend converted two 55-gallon drums into grills. Back then a bag of chicken leg quarters cost 19 cents a pound (they're 59 cents a pound now). I would buy two of three bags of chicken pieces, season them and then start cooking. Remember, I was out in the country, which has its obvious disadvantages for a restaurant, but also had a few advantages. There were no buildings around, only bushes. There were no houses, only trees. I didn't have to worry as much about obeying every health code and city regulation as I do now.

Some of my friends thought that I was crazy to try and operate that far out. They had a point, but, as always, I listened more to my instinct than to other people. I trusted prayer more than speculative advice.

My faith paid off. About six months after I'd moved to the new location, I saw construction crews begin to clear land and start to build on a hill in the land next to my place. The workers saw my shop and smelled the food being grilled right next to their daily work place. They ate it. They loved it. They spread the word. Soon people started stopping by from all around: Atlanta, Decatur, as far as Alpharetta. Business got so good that even the police were interested. One day a police car stopped by and a cop asked me what I was selling. He'd been driving by on his patrol route and had noticed the increase in cars in my place. He was curious, so I gave him a sample of Jerk Chicken to take back with him. A few days later I pulled into my restaurant and saw dozens of police cars there. I thought they might've been chasing some escaped fugitive, but they were just hungry. My life had started to turn around. I was making a name for myself and making Georgians happy and full of Jamaican food.

Then I moved again.

I move around a lot, don't I?

When an opportunity presents itself, I've always taken it. It's served me well.

MISS G AND THE THIEVES

Once again, I came to the crossroads. My first efforts to sell fish at an Atlanta restaurant had been thwarted by greed and jealousy. But, I'd been there before. I knew that there are always options. There was a woman I called Miss G who always bought fish from me for her store. This kindly lady let me set up shop in the parking lot in front of her store. It was a good move for both of us. Since I brought with me some loyal customers, her business increased. I sold fish there out of the back of my van for six months until some people called the police on me. The police informed me that I couldn't sell fish there, but Miss G let me continue to sell inside of her store.

I distinctly remember trying to warn Miss G about a certain scam artist who wanted to go into business with her, setting up a travel agency in a ghetto neighborhood in south Atlanta. Miss G was kind and a bit naïve. I had been burned in the past and tried to share some of my wisdom with her, but she went ahead with the venture, despite my warning that no one in that location could possibly afford to go on luxury vacations when they were all just struggling to pay their rent. In fact, Miss G told the con-woman about me and my warning, and she told Miss G to get rid of ME, which she did. So, yet again, I had to start over at square one.

I had a friend named Sue. She and I talked and came to the conclusion that there was only one fish market in Atlanta at the time. The two of us set up a market on Glenwood Avenue to sell to restaurants and hotels. When Sue eventually left the business, I partnered with another person. I realize now, looking back with clearer eyes, that I was simply repeating a pattern. I could see this destructive pattern outside of myself with others, like the incident with Miss G and the travel agency, but I could not see the exact same thing when it was happening to me. My father always told me that friendship and money don't mix, but I still hadn't learned that valuable lesson.

So, I teamed up with yet another partner, Winston. I had the idea, the equipment and a little money. He had a little money and no experience. I believed Winston to be a decent and honest man, which is why I agreed to let him go into business with me. We found another place which was already set up as a restaurant and set up a fish market outside of it. Kelly and Winston's Restaurant and Fish Market started off going great guns. We roared out of the gate. Every time I set up another fish market or restaurant I found success. People liked and wanted what I was selling. Business picked up and we were starting to do well. It was around the time that we were getting our first taste of success that Winston began to change. My mind and that nagging little voice kept telling me that I was going in the wrong direction, but my body was saying that I should go ahead with it anyway.

One day Winston and I got into an argument, about money of course. I was putting up my share of the money and Winston wasn't. Since my name wasn't on the business license, when Winston kicked me out, I was stuck. I had to start over…again.

Yes, I know that the pattern is pretty obvious now. They say that hindsight is 20/20, and it is. But that doesn't mean that it's easy to see these patterns when you are experiencing them.

HOW I CAME TO ATHENS

There's a popular alternative newspaper in Atlanta called *Creative Loafing*. I used to advertise my Atlanta restaurant within its pages. My contact at the paper called me once, and we talked about Jamaican restaurants up the road in Athens. I'd never heard of the Athens in Georgia. I knew about that Athens in Greece (that lesser Athens), but the college town up the road from Atlanta, the place which would become my beloved home, was, at the time, just a dot on the map to me. But my *Creative Loafing* representative and I had a good relationship, so I invited her to drop by my Atlanta area restaurant and try the food.

She did. After sampling some of my menu she commented that it wasn't very spicy. And she was right. My regulars in Atlanta didn't want their food spicy, and so I had dialed back the natural heat of traditional Jamaican food. She liked my food, but thought that it lacked the kick that spices, such as Scotch Bonnet, generally give Jamaican food.

One week later, I decided to take a trip to Athens and see what she was talking about. There was one small Jamaican restaurant (if you can even call it that). You may remember it, on Milledge Avenue, near the entrance to "The Loop." I'm not even sure if the word "restaurant" accurately describes it. It was more like a shack than a proper restaurant. There was no stove, limited seating, and the owner clearly didn't have much of a sense of the atmosphere she was trying to create. While I admit that I am completely biased, her food was pretty bad as well.

However, after talking to her, my mood changed drastically. She said that she was closing up shop, and wondered if I wanted to buy her restaurant and inherit the location. Sensing an opportunity, I jumped on it. Athenians already associated that location with Jamaican food. Mine is better. 2 + 2 = a whole mess of nonsense, but I didn't know that at the time.

It turns out that she was just trying to get out of her lease. A mere nine months after I opened the first Athens "Kelly's," she opened a competing restaurant on the other side of town. Still, I was determined to do it "my way" as I've always done. Despite her lying, some legal troubles with her which I won't go into, and my new, less than stellar, location, I asked that little voice for advice once again. "Put Me first and I will take you places you never dreamed of." That voice has never steered me wrong.

My first restaurant in Athens, on Milledge Avenue

Around six months after I opened I noticed that something wasn't right. Customers stopped coming, even after having complimented my food when they first tried it. I soon discovered that my new nemesis had been spreading false rumors about me. I could've sunk to her level and fought back, but that wouldn't be what The Voice told me to do. Instead, I kept plugging away and looking for new opportunities to get my food in front of noses and mouths.

Athens used to have an annual event, "The Taste of Athens," where restaurateurs cook dishes for the community. It's heavily publicized and has been known to make or break local restaurants. This was my moment. I knew that my nemesis was going to be there. I knew that I could make infinitely better food than she did. And I knew a few tricks of the trade (like making fresh food and keeping it warm so that tasters aren't forced to eat old meals). I came late to the event, on purpose, because I wanted to serve fresh food to hungry diners, preferably after they'd had a few drinks and were in a good mood. One man who tried and was over the moon about my Jerk texted all of his friends to come…and by the end of the night I had secured my place in town as the premier Jamaican restaurant owner.

It wasn't long before I was the only local Jamaican restaurant owner. She closed down not long after the Taste of Athens. As always, I learned some valuable lessons that day:

Work hard.
Work harder than your competition.
Keep the faith.
Believe in yourself.
Revenge is a dish best served fresh.

SECRETS THAT <u>THEY</u> DON'T WANT YOU TO KNOW

You don't need to buy those expensive medicines they try to sell on TV ads. A little old country wisdom works better, costs less, and doesn't have all of those side-effects. My mother knew a lot of these "home remedies." Bragg's Apple Cider Vinegar and Aloe are the closest things to miracle panaceas there are. Yes, Aloe is the same stuff they use to heal wounds. You only want to ingest a little, but it helps with everything from sinus problems to cancer. Unlike chemotherapy, my cures are easy. Step One—take two drops of Bragg's and add them to a glass of distilled water. Step Two—drink it.

The Aloe cure needs real Aloe, the plant, not some concocted lotion with added ingredients. Step One—cut a stalk in half, cut off the edges of the plant, peel back the skin, removing the spikes. Step Two—Soak it in water overnight. Step Three—mix with a tea, juice or whatever and drink. DO NOT LET IT SOAK FOR TOO LONG. It will sour.

Lime and water lessens high blood pressure. My mother used this cure and, although she also sometimes tried the medicine the doctors gave her, lime and water worked better. It's equally as easy to prepare.

You can boil impurities from water. Campers do it with soiled river water. In Jamaica we had fresher tap water than here in the States, though some of the news stories about unhealthy tap water are just marketing tricks to get you to buy bottled water for a dollar fifty, or whatever ludicrous amount of money they're now charging for something that covers two-thirds of the planet.

I don't eat black pepper. It doesn't fully digest and builds up in your kidneys, leading to kidney stones.

I also don't drink Coke or Pepsi. They're just water, sugar and a bunch of chemicals you don't want to know about.

LEARNED AT MY FATHER'S KNEE

I learned a lot from my father. He and I were not as close once I'd grown up as we had been when I was little. I admired his faith. Even his death reinforced my faith in God. He always said that he was going to keep on living until he saw a black president of the United States. He died in February of 2009, just one month after Barack Obama was sworn in as America's 44th president. We were together the month before, sitting outside his home in Jamaica. I remember he told me, "Boy, pour me a drink." I did, and I poured myself one, too. We sat together one last time as father and son. After a few drinks, he leaned back and mused, "Now I've seen it all…a black president of the United States of America." He was a stubborn man, and I thank God that he passed that trait on to me.

My parents were married for 60-something years. That's a long time. They fought, sure, but divorce was simply never an option.

Once my father caught me stealing money from our family store to spend on junk food (cake, candy, the stuff kids crave). When I was caught, my father didn't beat me, not this time. Stealing was too serious for that punishment. Instead he grabbed me by the collar, dragged me to the nearest tree and tied my hands and feet to the trunk. He tied me to a tree. That's a lesson you don't forget. Luckily, after a good while my brother saw me and untied me. I didn't steal from the family store after that.

ENTREPRENUERIAL SPIRIT

I wanted to share a few tips I've learned over the years. A large part of what has made me a successful businessman is not giving up and a willingness to try new things. Business, like life, throws you curveballs. You have to have the attitude of perseverance or, without a doubt, you will fail.

Since opening my first restaurant, I've never been satisfied with just minding the store. When the opportunity arose to open a second restaurant, I jumped at the chance. Every time that I'm given the chance to set up a tent and sell my food to new customers in new locations, I do it. They don't always immediately pay off, but I do it anyway. Down the road, they usually pay dividends.

The common wisdom is that ninety percent of restaurants close within a year. It's true, but I know why.

The answer is simple. Most restaurant owners don't know anything about cooking. They have to rely on a cook. Even truer than that is this: <u>Most failed restaurants have owners who don't have love in their hearts</u>.

You have to love the food you're cooking, otherwise what's the difference between selling food and selling lawn furniture. You have to love the idea of feeding people right. You have to love your employees (unless they prove themselves unworthy of your love, but even so, you've got to give them a chance). If you're just in the restaurant business to make money, you're not doing it right. You have to love what you do. Read any book about happiness. It will tell you the same.

Since, like most new businesses, you won't make money for a few years, you also have to have some cash reserves. That's it. Those are the two simple secrets to making it in the restaurant business: love and patience.

SOME OLD JAMAICAN SECRETS FROM THE FARM

I run restaurants. It helps in the food game if you know something about food. You'd think that that would be obvious, but look around at all of the awful restaurants out there that continue to serve unhealthy, artery-clogging, bland semi-food. Some of them are really successful, for various reasons. Personally, I've always felt that it's possible to serve healthy, quality food at a reasonable price. That plus customer service plus a little luck and prayer can equal success.

Ackee is the Jamaican national fruit. I know this contradicts what I just said, but it has a pretty bland taste. So, we islanders always mix it with something else. Ackee and saltfish is a popular dish. "Saltfish" in Jamaica means non-fresh fish. There are really only two categories of fish in Jamaica: fresh fish and saltfish. Fresh fish is, obviously, fish caught recently off shore. It IS an island after all. Saltfish is fish that's been shipped. It's usually white codfish, but not necessarily.

Allspice, or pimenta, is one of those spices we put in everything. We use the leaves to line our cook pits. We use the spice to add flavor to our meals. Like the American Indian of the plains and the buffalo, no part of the pimenta plant goes to waste in Jamaica.

My mother came to America in the 1960s when farm prices took a tumble. We Jamaicans know how to adjust to any situation. In that turbulent decade a lot of the traditional Jamaican exports weren't demanded like they had been previously. Pumpkins, yams, banana and, of course, sugar cane, markets took a nose dive. My family was a farm family. Sure, we had a store and my dad had been a butcher, but everything had revolved around the farming. It was family tradition. It wasn't easy for my father to give up his life's work, but his lessons are still around in me and my brothers. With my restaurants, I've tried to bring that tradition into the twenty-first century while still maintaining the purity of the food and the cooking process. It's not easy, but it's worth it. With every meal I prepare, I'm honoring my ancestors.

TRUE BELIEF CAN COME IN THE FORM OF VAN

Sometimes one small change can alter everything else in your life. One minor adjustment can have huge ripple effects. For me, this change came in the form of a white van.

It sounds like no big deal, but as soon as I bought the large, white van I still have today, my business took off and my horizons opened. I was able to transport my grill, my food, and my serving trays to outdoor festivals, to street fairs, and to catering events. I was able to go to market and bring my food back to my restaurant myself, without delivery trucks.

I needed a means of transportation. I needed a way to expand my business. I needed a way to take over some of the chores that I had relied on others to perform. And so, I prayed for it. I asked for help. I received it.

I got the van right before I moved the restaurant from the end of Milledge Avenue to Five Points. As soon as I got the van, it felt as if everything I'd been hoping and praying for simply fell into place.

If you look at it, it's just a plain white van. It can't fly. It doesn't have the power of teleportation. It's not a time machine. It's just a van. And yet, it completely changed my life.

JUST SOME MORE UNCONNECTED THOUGHTS

1---CURIOSITY---The Hubble Space Telescope was an incredible human invention. We launched this observational miracle into space. It took some amazing shots of outer space. Then it got too close to a black hole, got sucked in, and is now gone (or somewhere else). We'll probably never know the true fate of Hubble. But there is a lesson about curiosity and a cat and a bad ending for him coming to mind.

2---TIME---Bowen and I talked about the concept of time. I told him that, for half of the year, Jamaica is on Eastern Standard Time and, therefore, when it's noon in New York City or Miami, then it's also noon in Kingston or Montego Bay. But, in Jamaica, there is no "daylight savings time" and so, for the other half of the year, we're an hour off. Bowen was ranting about Congress having the power to control time. I noticed that he was about to go off onto a lengthy rant about power, corruption and greed. I cut him off. I told him, "They can't control time. Time keeps moving. They don't control time. They just control the clock." It seemed to shut him up.

3---WE KELLYS HAVE TO STICK TOGETHER---Since my restaurant is named "Kelly's" I have a lot of people who share my name posing for pictures under my sign. I like this. I don't know why I like it, but I do.

4---INSURANCE---The University of Georgia football team has a devoted, sometimes rabid, fan base. Georgia fans have been known to travel halfway around the country to cheer on their team. There are some intense rivalries that play out each and every year. One of UGA's biggest rivals is the University of Florida, "The Gators." It's tradition that UGA and UF play their annual game in Jacksonville, Florida, basically in between the homes of both of these schools. One of the biggest events of the year for any Athenian is the "Georgia-Florida game," also known, appropriately, as "The World's Biggest Outdoor Cocktail Party." Well, cocktail parties need food. I make and sell food. I'm always up for setting up a tent or a booth in different locations to entice hungry people to try Jamaican food. So, one year, I made the trip to Jacksonville. I packed my van and hitched the grill to the back of my van, then set off for Jacksonville. When I arrived, I was told by the city that I needed to have a license and have two million dollars worth of insurance before I could even set up a tent. It's a hurricane thing. Much like the Caribbean, the coast of Florida gets hit with the wrath of the sea often. I couldn't afford the insurance and was, frankly, a little disgusted with the fact that they needed me to have it in the first place. So, I repacked and headed down to Miami to see my mother. As fate would have it, southern Florida had just been hit by yet another hurricane. So, I set out my tent on the streets of Miami and gave away food to hurricane victims.

5---FAITH HEALING---I've been a true believer all of my life. I've been a searcher, checking out different faiths and different practitioners of these faiths. I've watched a lot of TV preachers doing their thing. I know that he's known and remembered mainly for hypocrisy, but I really liked Jimmy Swaggart. I believe in faith healing. I know that a lot of mainstream Christians like to make fun of it, but I truly believe that if you believe strongly in something, you can do amazing things, even curing your own bodily ailments.

OTHER PEOPLE'S THOUGHTS ABOUT ME

I have an anniversary party for my customers once a year. It's on April 20th. Go ahead and make your jokes. I'm Jamaican. I've heard them all before. I swear that the date was a coincidence, not that I don't play the inside joke up a bit as a friendly tie between me and my wonderful customers. Anyway, the point is, I have an annual Customer Appreciation Day at my restaurants. There are lunch and dinner specials, a DJ spinning island tunes, even a live broadcast from a local Caribbean music internet radio station. Since I was going to be understandably busy that day, I sent my devoted little publisher out with his notepad to interview some of the people who stopped by this past year. He got a few quotations about me and my food:

Owner of Beachhits.com --- "I needed a voice for liner work on my station and I was already a fan of Kelly's food. So I called him and went to his place. We talked and I loved him. You can't help but hit it off when you meet Kelly. I knew that he had a great voice, but it wasn't until later that I realized that everybody already knew Kelly. People ask me if that's his voice on the radio."

<u>Patrick Roach, party DJ and musician, from Stone Mountain</u> ---"It's the best Jerk Chicken ever. Totally worth the drive. I've known Kelly for fifteen years. We met at a soccer field in Lithonia. He's just the kind of man you want to be around."

<u>Local customer, young professional with four year old son in tow, introducing his son to Jamaican food for the first time, talking about Kelly's success</u> ---"He's an honest fellow. He's very humble and welcoming. Why aren't all restaurants like Kelly's?"

<u>Local college student, regular at Kelly's</u> ---"I eat here all the time. I've never seen him angry. He's always pleasant, soft-spoken and fair. It's such a relief compared to everyone else."

<u>J.J., woman new to town</u> --- "Kelly was the first person I met in Athens. I felt a little lost until I met him. Now I feel like I'm home."

LIKE FAMILY, EXCEPT I PAY THEM

A large portion of this book is devoted to what I consider good, learned-through-hard-experience advice about sound business practice. If you've read this far, you probably already know that. One of the biggest lessons I've learned is to <u>surround yourself with good people and you will all win in the end</u>. It may sound obvious. It's definitely been said many times before. But the reason that it's a cliché is that it's worked so many times before.

I'm a trusting soul. I try to give everyone a chance. When it comes to employees, I've hired workers in the past who other employers wouldn't have given a second glance. I've also hired workers who look great on paper. The fact is that some of the people from both categories have worked out and some haven't. Unlike Jerk Chicken, I don't have the perfect recipe for what makes the ideal employee. Some people are great during the interview process and wind up failing. Some people are awful at selling themselves and wind up being loyal, attentive, eager employees. Some people will steal from you. Other people won't. And you simply cannot always tell who is going to wind up in which category. I stick by my lifelong stance of giving everyone a chance. It's simple fairness.

I'm a kind man. It's just fact that some opportunistic people with evil in their hearts will always mistake kindness for weakness. They will try and take advantage of kind people. Wall Street crooks and Ponzi schemers don't try and fleece their fellow criminals. They lie and steal from the kind and the hopeful. I've hired a few of them. I'll give anyone a chance. But even my patience has its limits.

I've had dozens of employees over the years. I've hired Jamaicans. I've hired Americans. I've hired black people. I've hired white people. I've hired men. I've hired women. I've hired strangers. I've hired family. And the people I want to mention here have now all become "like family" to me.

I wanted to write a little about some of my long-term employees who have stuck it out and have been efficient, loyal, and helpful. They've made my restaurants what they are, happy places with not only great food, but great atmospheres where people want to stay, have a drink, talk with me or with their friends, listen to some music, and laugh. I'm extremely proud whenever I see returning customers, people who may only come to Athens once or twice a year, but, when they do, they always make a point of stopping in Kelly's. Without the people I'm about to write about, that might not be the case. They're like family.

TERESA:

I've known Teresa for well over a decade. She used to come by my place on Milledge Avenue and talk. I knew her long before she came to work for me. She worked for years at another traditional Athens eatery, Wilson's Soul Food. Teresa came to me with the knowledge of how to cook mouth-watering barbecue pork that falls off the bone, how long to boil them and how big a "ham hock" to throw in there in order to bring out the flavor in your greens, and how to talk to customers and treat them like family. I guess she was just born with that gift.

I had just had to fire an employee who was stealing from me, and so I needed some help in a hurry. Although I hadn't seen her in a few years, I immediately thought of Teresa. The lady can cook. I liked her. I knew that she was trustworthy. I asked a mutual friend to get me in touch with her. Teresa came in the next day. We talked. I hired her on the spot. Her transition from soul food to Jamaican food was relatively easy. Although there are some distinct differences in the styles (especially the spicing), there are also a lot of similarities. Both styles like to let the spices lay and soak into the meat. Both styles like to take their time. The American barbecue and the Jamaican "Out Kitchen" are roughly the same idea. You let the meat slow-roast. You trap the heat and let the smell do its work making hungry folks hungrier. And the uses of the food are similar, too. It brings people together for good times.

Although she's only worked for me for a little over a year, I trust Teresa completely. She's in charge of my second restaurant when I'm not there. Like all of my longtime employees, she talks to the customers. She makes them feel welcome, and this lets them know that eating at

102

Kelly's is about more than eating at some faceless fast-food chain restaurant. It's about people. I'm proud that Teresa is one of those people.

MISS P:

That's not her Christian name, but everybody who's ever met her has always called her Miss P. Miss P has been with me for five years now, since I had the restaurant on Baxter Street. She was with me when we were located at the end of Milledge, near the on-ramp to The Loop, and she came with me when we moved to our current Five Points location.

Miss P is quite possibly the sweetest woman in the world. She personifies the phrase "like family." She's one of the only cooks I trust to season the meat. Her goodness and humility shine out of her like a saint. She might be a saint. I'll call The Vatican and see. If preparing some of the world's best Jerk Pork isn't officially considered one of the three miracles necessary for sainthood, it darn well should be.

Miss P just walked into my life one day. She strolled into the restaurant and asked for a job, just like anyone else. I had a good feeling about her, but, like I say, I'm a trusting sort. I've had good feelings about the dozens of no-good employees who turned out to be lazy or thieves. I was suspicious of her at first, merely because I'd been burned by employees before. I called her the day after she came into my restaurant. She's been with me every since. I feel a little guilty even mentioning laziness or thievery in the same paragraph as Miss P. She's that decent a lady. I can barely refer to her as a woman since the title "lady" fits her so well.

SANDY:

She's my cousin. You can't walk into my Five Points location without seeing her honest smile and big shimmering brown eyes, full of love and happiness. Working with family members sometimes is the best idea in the world. Sometimes it's the worst. Working with Sandy was one of the best decisions of my professional life.

We communicate so well that some might say that we've got a telepathic connection. She knows what I need sometimes before I even realize I need it. She's been a reliable and helpful worker since the day she started working with me. And there's no doubt that her bubbly personality and her beauty (inside and out) is one of the keys to my continued success. Men do stand at the counter and flirt with her, sometimes for hours on end. Who could blame them? She is a beautiful woman with a heart of gold. I couldn't design a better cousin if I were a Japanese engineer putting together the ideal worker.

MY LANDLORD:

My landlord, Billy Slaughter, and I have gotten close. He owns the property at Five Points where my main restaurant is now located. But we've got more than your usual renter-landlord relationship. I consider him a friend. We go out for coffee almost every Saturday morning at the Jittery Joe's coffee shop across the street from my place and we talk for hours. He rents the space next to mine, a national sandwich chain restaurant. They're a successful chain and they pay their bills on time. I do, too, and I've been able to show my landlord that local restaurants are better tenants, not only because the food is much better than the chains, but because, unlike the chains, we add flavor to the local scene. We enhance the atmosphere and create a place for people to make memories. In fact, one year when I was about to renew my lease, he had a chance to rent the property to another national chain, and he didn't because he wanted to keep Athens unique and not let it look and feel like every other town. I'm extremely proud that I was able to show this intelligent and successful man that good business and local flavor can go hand-in-hand.

PS --- Mister Slaughter passed away while we were writing this book. He will be missed.

LESTER:

Lester is a good friend. He has always been supportive of me and my efforts. He recently moved to Houston, which unfortunately is in Texas, but I still wish my friend Lester well.

GOD IS LOVE

In case you haven't guessed by now, I'm a believer. I was raised to love the Lord and I still do. I've struggled all my life to understand the mystery of God. I attended a Seventh Day Adventist high school. These days, I don't attend church services regularly, but, honestly, I believe that not attending church has given me more time and energy to devote to actually thinking about God. I'm not trying to put down any church-goers. My grandmother was a regular attendee, and she's the holiest, kindest woman I've ever known in my life. If going to church works for you, great, but if not, that doesn't mean that you can't love the Lord.

I wanted to write a chapter about my own thoughts on the holiest of holies. I'm not a theologian. I'm not a preacher. I'm not even one of those guys on TV with the hair-dos that never move, those guys who keep the hair spray industry in business. I'm just a man who's thought a lot about the big mysteries of life.

Some people think that mankind is inherently evil. Some say that it's because of Adam and Eve in the Garden of Eden. Others just read history books and see that we've done some awful stuff to each other throughout the ages. I'm more of an optimist. I believe that most people are decent, and I say this after having lived for sixty some years and after having seen and lived through betrayal by those closest to me, some of the most horrific racism the world has ever seen (thanks, Texas), people killing people for no good reason, people stealing and raping and lying and generally not being human to each other. Still, I remain an opti-mist. Remember, Satan was once an angel. When God kicked Satan out of heaven, Satan taunted God. Of course the devil was a smack-talker. But God said to Satan, "Don't think that all of those people down there belong to you. Some of them belong to me." Satan's powerful. I know that. But, he's not as powerful as God. God is great. God is everywhere. God is love.

AND NOW, WHAT YOU'VE ALL BEEN WAITING FOR

My life story is pretty exciting. I know. I've lived it. But, if you knew and loved me even before buying this book, I'll admit that it's probably because of my food. I've cooked traditional Jamaican delicacies for more UGA graduating classes than I can count. I've cooked for artists, firemen, doctors, janitors, businessmen, homeless men, barbers, babies, construction workers, college professors, and college drop-outs. Some people come to my restaurants because they love the atmosphere at Kelly's. Other people come because they love the reasonable prices, generous portions and the convenience. But everyone loves the taste.

Everyone wants the recipes to my food. About once a day someone asks me for the recipe for Jerk Chicken. I'm not exaggerating.

Customers want to know how to make spicy cabbage, spicy squash, Jerk Pork, and my Jamaican-style cornbread. I wanted to include a special treat for anyone who buys my book. I'm not going to "give away the store," as they say here in the States, but I will tell you a few of my secrets, learned at my grandmother's knee when I was just a wee thing.

I'm going to give you a little history about my cooking philosophy, and then I'll lay out a couple of recipes. I'll take it slow. Americans aren't used to some of the more exotic island dishes, like oxtail, "Dip and Fall Back," or Run-Down, but the philosophy behind all Jamaican food is the same:

THE SECRET IS NOT TO MEASURE.

That may sound ridiculous, seeing as I'm about to give you recipes, but I'm not going to give you detailed amounts of ingredients because cooking isn't like building a car. It's not a science. It's an art. My grandmother never owned a measuring cup. She'd dash-and-taste, dash-and-taste. She'd throw a dash of tarragon into the pot, stir it, pull out the big wooden spoon, bring it to her lips, and sample it. She learned how to cook the island way. You keep mixing and tasting until you get it right. Actually, by the time I came along, she'd been doing it for so long that she pretty well knew the correct amounts of different ingredients to add to her usual recipes, but when she cooked something new, I'd still see her go back to the old dash-and-taste.

I tell people that I never measure, but that's not entirely true. The only thing I measure for is cake. I'll admit that when I'm baking a cake I follow the recipe to the letter and do as the instructions tell me to do. That's full disclosure for you lucky readers. But, with that one exception, I don't measure.

THE OLD WAYS ARE BETTER

The invention of the microwave may have made cooking faster, but it also made cooking infinitely worse. Taste has suffered thanks to technology. I do have gas stoves at my restaurants, but I also make sure that I stay true to my grandmother's teaching and have an "Out-Kitchen." I told you a little about out-kitchens earlier in the book. Cooking over burning embers of wood adds a flavor to meat that simply cannot be duplicated.

In my first Athens location at the end of Milledge Avenue (near The Loop, for you Athenians and UGA alums), my little building was nothing more than a tiny rental space with a shack out back. Even though it was a bit of a step-down from my place in Stone Mountain, I knew that I had to start at the bottom again, taking a step back so that I could later take two steps forward. The place didn't come with anything other than a steam table, a regular electric house stove, some chairs and a table. There was no exhaust system, and no commercial stove of any kind, but I made sure that there was a shack out back before I rented the space. The space was much smaller and more cramped than either of my current spaces, but it had character, and, just as important, it had a shack out back that I used as an out-kitchen for grilling.

My grandmother didn't cook anything inside of the house and I will always stay true to her legacy. She didn't believe in cooking indoors. She believed in the old ways. She believed in firewood. Trust me. I was the one who wound up fetching most of the wood. At the beginning of the week, I always had to make sure that she had enough wood for an entire week's cooking. Cooking with firewood made the food taste so much better. Let me repeat that. Cooking with firewood made the food taste so much better. Most food doesn't actually taste like much of anything (and I'm not just talking about ackee and saltfish, but that is a good example). Here comes another secret:

IT'S THE SEASONING THAT GIVES FOOD THE TASTE

To prove my point, I'm going to show you how to cook one of my most popular dishes, Jamaican Spicy Cabbage. By itself, cabbage is a pretty tasteless food, but...

Spicy Cabbage Cheat Sheet

WHAT YOU NEED
1 Cabbage
1 Onion, regular sized
½ Red Bell Pepper
½ Green Bell Pepper
2 Hot Peppers (Scotch Bonnet)
1 cup of Honey
¼ teaspoon of Salt
¼ teaspoon of Paprika

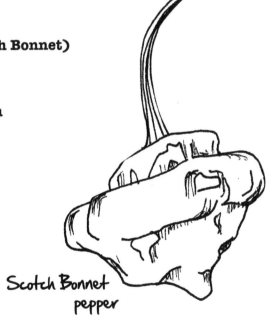

Scotch Bonnet
pepper

DIRECTIONS

1. Get a head of cabbage and wash it. Cut the cabbage in two equal halves.

2. Cut out the heart. Slice the cabbage in about five or six equally-sized slices before dicing it.

3. Get a small skillet or pot. Put the cabbage in the small pot with a little salt and water (not too much) and bring it to boil.

4. Get your veggies: red and green bell peppers, onion, and one hot pepper (or two, depending on how spicy you like it). I use the island treat, Scotch Bonnet (remember, I warned you about Scotch Bonnet earlier in the book. It's not as hot as Ghost Pepper or Scorpion Pepper, but it is hot, so be warned.). Cut up all of the peppers and onions.

5. Add a little oil to the pot and then add the cut up vegetables. Add the seasonings of your choice. Experiment. It's fun.

6. Fry for two or three minutes.

7. Drain the water from the cabbage while it's still hot and add the seasonings. There's still going to be some water retained by the cabbage even after draining, but that's okay.

8. Add the seasoning. Add the honey. Then add some paprika to give it even more kick.

9. Stir well with a spoon until everything mixes together.

10. Keep it hot until serving if you can. Fresher is always better.

11. Eat. Enjoy.

Jamaican Spicy Squash

Spicy Squash Cheat Sheet

WHAT YOU NEED

2 Yellow Squash

2 Zucchini

1 Onion, regular sized

½ Red Bell Pepper

½ Green Bell Pepper

1 Hot Pepper (again I've got to suggest Scotch Bonnet or my parents will disown me, but they're not your parents, so do what you like)

1 cup of Honey

¼ teaspoon of Salt

¼ teaspoon of Paprika

¼ cup of Oil

DIRECTIONS

1. Cut the squash and zucchini into little circles and then set it aside for a bit.

2. Dice the red and green peppers, the onion, and the hot pepper.

3. Put it all into a frying pan with oil and fry for about two to three minutes.

4. Add the squash, the zucchini, the paprika, the salt, and the honey to the frying pan, along with ¼ of a cup of water.

5. Stir for two to three minutes then turn the stove down low.

6. Let it cook slow for five minutes.

7. Then turn the stove off and let it sit for another ten minutes.

8. Eat. Smile.

JERK…MORE THAN A DISH, A WAY OF LIFE

There is no food more associated with Jamaica than Jerk. Jerk Chicken and Jerk Pork are the most popular imports into the USA, but back home we Jerk everything. We make Jerk Fish. We make Jerk Shrimp. When we're out of real food, we make Jerk Spam.

You name it and we can Jerk it in Jamaica.

I'm going to give you some Jerk recipes in a few pages, and they're two of my staple dishes. They're the lunch and dinner options that people crave and dream about. Along with

This is how it's done

the spices and the atmosphere, they're what has made my restaurants successful. First, though, since Jerk is so synonymous with Jamaican food, I need to give you a bit of Jerk history and some Jerk philosophy. Also, I need to tell you a little about how I started to be a jerk.

From what I've heard, jerking meat started in either Port Royal or Portland, both coastal cities on my island. I don't know. I'm not even sure that anyone actually knows where Jerk began, but there are many theories. Wherever it began, it didn't stay there long. Anywhere you go in Jamaica you're going to find a Jerk spot. It's on the north coast, the south coast, the east coast and the west coast. It's in fancy restaurants at posh resorts. It's in ramshackle road side stands on the streets of Kingston. Its smell permeates the country dirt roads of the mountains and the busy congested streets of the cities.

Jerk is not just getting a cut of meat and putting it in the pan. Like all Jamaican food, like all food period, the secret is in the seasoning: Scotch Bonnet Peppers, scallions, thyme, allspice, brown sugar, browning sauce, soy sauce. I use all of them. The soy or browning sauce gives not only flavor but also a little color. Walkerswood Jerk Seasoning is a popular brand. When I started, I used it myself until I had time to develop my own special recipe.

A SHORT HISTORY OF HOW I BECAME A JERK

<u>Opening a restaurant is a dream that I never dreamed of dreaming</u>.

I didn't come to America thinking of opening up a restaurant. As a younger man I had absolutely no idea that I'd make a living doing something my grandmother taught me. I attended business school, but, at the time, I assumed that I would go in a more traditional business and wind up in one of any number of fields, like accounting or book keeping. I pictured myself in some sort of office. But, I've always been a risk-taker. I've always been willing to try something new, something different. A child born right now might expect to have five or six distinct, separate careers in his life, but when I was born most people had one job and held it all of their lives. I guess that makes me forward-thinking. That sounds much better than describing myself as a guy who gets bored easily.

You know that I've moved around a lot in my life. I've always had that nomadic spirit. It was easy for me to pick up and move: Texas, Virginia, Washington, DC, Florida, Georgia. My first restaurant was in Georgia, outside of Atlanta, but, if I'm tracing the history of this dream I never dreamed of dreaming, then it probably started when I was in Florida. I saw that no one was transporting fresh fish from the Florida coast to inland metropolises like Atlanta, so I did that. I've never understood people who put their dreams on hold. You want to do something; you just put on your pants, jump in and do it. That's how I got into the fresh fish transport business. I bought and sold the fish in Atlanta. I realized that I could cut out the middleman and just sell the fish myself, so I did that. I discovered that no one in Atlanta was cooking real Jamaican Jerk, so I opened a Jerk stand on Covington Highway, cooking savory Jerk Chicken and Fish. When I started in Atlanta, there were a few restaurants PRETENDING to cook Jerk. They were just baking chicken and pork plain and then adding a few spices after it cooked. I went to a Jamaican place with a friend and we sampled their lame attempts at island food. I said that it was just plain chicken with generic Jerk sauce. My friend, who'd sampled my Jerk before, said that I could make a killing. So, I tried that. I had a welder friend make me a grill out of fifty-five gallon drum. It took him about a week. I found a place and researched the permits and all the legal stuff. Then I opened my doors. It helped that chicken prices were low then. When I started, I could buy a ten-pound bag of chicken for $1.90 and now it costs 60 cents a pound.

I've said before that my first place was really just a little hut on what was then a rural road out in the suburbs of a big city. It's not an exaggeration. I passed all the inspections, but it was little more than a roadside stand. But that didn't matter. The love and the food was what mattered.

Word of mouth is still the best advertising option in the world, especially for restaurants. Rumors of delicious Jamaican food spread throughout metro Atlanta and its suburbs. People came from Decatur, Stone Mountain, DeKalb County, Rockdale County, Cobb County, even as far as Alpharetta. After less than two months, I had so much business that I had to get my friend to make another grill, a bigger one. Even the DeKalb Police Department was curious. They wanted to know why the traffic was so heavy around my place. They probably thought that I was selling weed. People can be so stereotypical. But, as soon as they tasted my Jerk, they not only satiated their curiosity, but they filled their stomachs as well. When one of them took some Jerk back to the station, I knew that I was golden. My restaurant must've been a frequent guest star on the police radio, because I soon had a huge following of cops from all around the city.

I had such a large immediate following that I soon had a spy. There was a guy who became a regular at my first place. He befriended me and used to watch me cook while we talked. When I found out that he was just spying and was planning on opening up his own place, I banned him from the kitchen. He did eventually open up his own place, but, once again, my intuition had served me well. He was a nice guy, but I had that pit-of-the-stomach feeling when I first met him that something was off, and so I never let him learn all of my Jerk secrets, even when he was in the kitchen with me. His Jerk was bad and his restaurant didn't last very long. His spices were wrong, and, more importantly, he forgot the main ingredient.

He forgot to add the love.

The seasoning depends on the amount of chicken, pork, or the number of wings.

WHAT YOU NEED

3 to 4 Scotch Bonnet Peppers

½ of a bunch of Thyme

½ of a bunch of Scallions

2 to 3 Onions

¼ of a cup of Allspice

½ of a teaspoon of Cinnamon Powder

¼ of a teaspoon of Nutmeg

¼ of a teaspoon of Salt

½ of a cup of Brown Sugar

¼ of a cup of Soy Sauce (for color)

WHAT TO DO WITH ALL OF THAT

1. Put everything in a food processor or a blender.

2. Add a little water to loosen it all up a little.

3. Blend.

4. Wash the chicken, pork or the wings.

5. Put the seasoning on the meat.

6. Rub the seasoning on the meat.

7. Let it marinate overnight.

8. It's ready to grill the next day, so grill it.

9. Eat. Enjoy.

Jamaican allspice

Oxtail

WHAT YOU NEED

2 to 3 pounds of Oxtail

1 Onion

2 to 3 stems of Thyme

¼ of a teaspoon of Seasoning Salt

¼ of a cup of Soy Sauce

DIRECTIONS

1. Wash and prepare your oxtail in a pot and add all ingredients.
2. Add cold water to your oxtail(s).
2. Cook on medium heat.
3. Add more water if needed.
4. Cook until the meat is tender.
5. Taste (if you like it hot, add a hot pepper).

Thyme

Rice & Peas

We call it Rice & Peas in the islands. It's called Rice & Beans here. Either way, it's the same dish.

WHAT YOU NEED

1 can of Coconut Cream

1 Onion (blended)

½ teaspoon of Salt

¼ of a cup of Oil

2 to 3 stems of Thyme

2 lb. bags of Kidney Beans

DIRECTIONS

1. Put the beans into two cups of cold water.

2. Bring to a boil.

3. Add more cold water to the beans to let the beans go to the bottom of the pot.

4. There is an old way to check and see if the beans are cooked: You can spoon 2 or 3 beans out and see if they mash into a paste.

5. Add all of your ingredients.

6. Stir the rice and beans together until everything is properly mixed.

7. Turn the stove down low.

8. Cover with foil for it to steam.

9. Check to make sure it's ready, that the rice is fully cooked (if the rice isn't fully cooked, add a little more water, recover with foil and steam until it's ready).

MAC & CHEESE

Children love macaroni and cheese. You may think that this is an American phenomenon given to us at a relatively cheap rate by the good people at Kraft, but that's not the way food comes to us. Big food companies, like Kraft, see pre-existing foods that people already like and they gobble up the small companies. Then they market the food that they stole to us, all the while acting as if they were the Thomas Edison of children's culinary choices.

If you think that Mac & Cheese only comes in a rectangular box, you are wrong. There are hundreds of varieties of macaroni and cheese. I'll skip the standard cookbook ingredients listed separately from directions on this one since it's macaroni and cheese, which, even in Jamaica, is a simple dish aimed at children, but enjoyed by everyone. Here's mine:

Mac & Cheese

WHAT YOU NEED (amounts depend on how much you want to make)

Some Macaroni

Some Milk

Some Cheese (a lot of cheese)

Some Butter

Some Salt (to personal taste)

DIRECTIONS

1. Boil macaroni until the noodles are cooked.

2. Drain the water.

3. Add milk, a lot of cheese, a little butter, and seasoning.

4. Put everything on the fire for the cheese and butter to melt.

5. Stir while it's on the stove.

6. Once it starts to look like an actual dish, remove it from the fire, transfer it to a separate container (one that you can put in an oven).

7. Sprinkle a lot more cheese on top, and then put it in the oven.

8. Bake it in the oven (350-400 degrees) for 1-1/2 to 2 hours to get that nice crust on top.

Jamaican Salmon

Everyone loves Jamaican salmon. Islanders know how to cook fish.

WHAT YOU NEED

1 bottle of Caesar Salad Dressing

1 dash of Paprika

1 large Salmon Filet

1 Green Bell Pepper

1 Red Bell Pepper

1 Onion

2 Scotch Bonnet (or Habanera) Peppers

DIRECTIONS

1. Marinate your salmon filet in the Caesar Salad dressing for 5 to 10 minutes while adding the paprika.

2. Cut the onions and red and green peppers.

3. Take the salmon out of the sauce and put it on the grill (flipping it in the middle)---save the sauce.

4. Add your cut onions and peppers to the sauce and boil for 10 minutes.

5. Once the salmon is finished grilling, put it in a pan, add the sauce with the cut vegetables, and put the whole thing into the oven and cook for 30-45 minutes (300 degrees) until it's ready to eat.

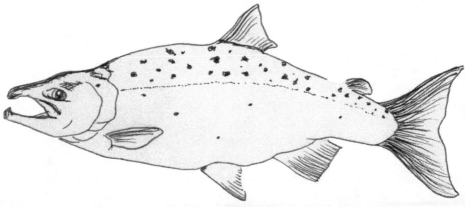

Curry Chicken

People get these ideas in their heads. They sit there, marinating. They harden with heat and time and, viola, you have a stereotype. People think that curry is only used in Indian cooking. That's crazy. Since the days of Marco Polo (the Italian explorer, not the swimming pool game of a similar name) spices have moved around quite a bit. Curry is quite popular in various pockets around the world. It can be used to flavor all kinds of meats, but most people prefer to use curry on chicken. I do.

Curry Chicken Cheat Sheet

WHAT YOU NEED

5 lbs. of Chicken

1 cup of White Vinegar

1 cup of Onions (sliced)

2 tablespoons of Curry Powder

½ tablespoon of Seasoning Salt (to personal taste)

1 can of Coconut Cream

WHAT TO DO WITH ALL OF THAT

1. Cut your chicken.

2. Wash it with vinegar and water.

3. Add your onions, some seasoning salt and curry powder into a sauce pan with a little water (too much will dilute the spices) -- use about a cup or two and add coconut cream.

4. Pour your sauce over the chicken and cook on a low fire.

5. Test to make sure that it is done.

6. Eat. Enjoy.

Escovitch Fish

This is an island staple. It's not super popular in the States, but I wanted to include at least one dish that will start you, the reader, on your way toward full-on Jamaican cooking, the stuff that sugar cane farmers, fishermen, janitors and prime ministers eat. I think I'll save most of those recipes for my second book.

WHAT YOU NEED

1 large Fish

1 Onion (sliced)

½ Green Bell Pepper (sliced)

½ Red Bell Pepper (sliced)

A dash of Paprika

1 Hot Pepper (once again, I prefer Scotch Bonnet, but there are many to choose from)

1 teaspoon of White Vinegar

1 teaspoon of Cooking Oil

DIRECTIONS

1. Fry your fish once and when it's done, set it aside.

2. Cut your onion and peppers.

3. Put onions and peppers into a skillet with a little oil and a little vinegar, add a dash of paprika, and stir until it's done (slightly sautéed).

4. Pour the mixture over your fried fish.

5. Eat. Enjoy.

JAMAICAN WORDS & SAYINGS

Since I only included a few Jamaican sayings in this book, I thought I'd make a short list of some of my favorite island phrases. We speak English in Jamaica. These are all English words and sayings. I swear. Feel free to use them in your everyday speech. No one will understand you, but they will think that you're a little cooler than you actually are.

Duppy: a ghost

True-true: authentic, real

Ting deh: a replacement for whatever you can't remember

Si mi?: Understand?

Skylark: idle, time wasted, sometimes used as an insult

Depon: plans

Blabba mout: someone who talks too much

Screechie: a complicated Jamaican dance move

Zeen: okay

Robut: an unlicensed bus or taxi

Obeah: black magic, a spell put on someone, or the description of the spell-caster

Drop-pan: a local gambling game

Bumboclaat: a curse phrase in surprise or anger

Butu: a disdainful slang term for a country person, implying stupidity

Chaka chaka: really messy, generally used judgmentally

JAMAICAN PATOIS PHRASES AND THEIR ENGLISH "TRANSLATIONS"

(with help from author Kathleen Wright,
retired medical practitioner and author of *At Full Bloom*)

Tidday fi mi tomorrow fi yuh (I am having a hard time now, but your rough time will also come)

Fram mi yeye de ah me knee (when I was very young)

Waata more dan flouwah (there is more to this than meets the eye)

Howdy and tenky nuh bruk nuh square (good manners cost nothing/so display them)

Ah nuh ebery ting dat 'ave sugah sweet (there are some things that are not what they may seem to be)

Nuh trubble trubble, till trubble trubble yuh (do not go looking for trouble)

Ef yuh sleep wid dawg yuh ketch im flea (if you keep bad company you will learn bad habits)

Puss nuh bisniss inna dawg fight (if a dispute does not concern you do not get involved)

Si mi an cum live wid mi a two differant ting (Knowing someone and living with them can change your good opinion of them)

Duppy know who fi frighten (bullies know how to pick their victims)

Every mikkle mek ah mukkle (every little bit counts)

Wah sweet nanny goat ah guh run 'im belly (the consequences of a secret pleasure may be regretted in the future)

Mi deh yah (I am here)

Mi ga'an (I am gone…I am leaving)

Bad like yaws (very bad)

Big bout yah (very important)

Hush yuh moute (be quiet)

Duppy conqueror (someone who has overcome an extreme event or experience)

Fallow fashin (copy cat)

Broughtupsy (upbringing)

Babylon (police/ politician who exploits people)

Dread (rastaman)

Dreadlocks (hair of the rastaman)

Bawn back ah cow (someone who displays stupid behavior)

Weh yuh ah deal wid (what are you doing?)

Weh yuh ah sey (what are you saying?)

Nutten nah gwaan (nothing is happening)

Yeouw (hey)

Wah gwaan (what is happening?)

Lickle more (until then)

Ital (natural food cooking style/salt free)

Irie (good)

I man (me)

KELLY'S "THOUGHT FOR TODAY"
(still hangs in his Five Points restaurant,
given to him by an unnamed Stone Mountain resident)

There is a curve called FAILURE...

A loop called CONFUSION...

Speed bumps called FRIENDS...

Red lights called ENEMIES...

Caution lights called FAMILY...

You will have flats called JOBS...But...

If you have a spare called DETERMINATION...

An engine called PERSEVERANCE...

Insurance called FAITH...

A drive called JESUS...

You will make it to a place called SUCCESS.

WORDS OF WISDOM...I HOPE

It may be a little cliché to hear some of these phrases. Some of them have been repeated for years, in various different ways, in every language on the planet. But that doesn't mean that they don't have value. There's a reason they've been repeated so often.

KELLY ON STARTING A BUSINESS:
"A business is like a woman having a baby. You have to give it time in the womb, time to become real. Then you've got to nurture it, let it grow in the right way. Maybe in twenty years you can take a break and stop being the parent, maybe."

"Business is always changing, always in flux. People ask me all the time how I stay afloat in business. They assume that I must have some huge storehouse of money and that I must have started out with a lot of money or else how could I have started a business? Those people can't see the forest for the trees. You don't need a heap of money to start something. You DO need a dream and the tenacity to see it through."

"A dream without money is the best kind of dream. A dream with money is just a plan. Where's the magic in that?"

KELLY ON CUSTOMER SERVICE:
"You can't have customers complain. It's about them. They're always right, even when they're not."

"With your employees, you are the boss. That means that, to them, you're always wrong. Of course, they're wrong a lot, too. The only person in business who is right is the customer."

KELLY ON BEING THE BOSS:
"When you're the boss, it's your business. The people who work for you won't always respect you. That's just the way humans work. But you can't just be their friend, not if you want to succeed."

133

"I wash dishes. I sweep floors. I set an example by doing every job in the store."

"My father taught me that you have to be able to do everything. If you want to run a business, you have to know how to do each and every job in the store. One of your workers is going to call in sick. Unless you only employ robots, it's inevitable. So, you've got to be able to fill in wherever is needed."

"I've taught the people who sell me meat how to do THEIR jobs before. I saw that they weren't cutting the meat the right way. So, I showed them how to do it the right way. They might not have liked me in the moment, but now they know how to do their jobs."

SOME BUSINESS ADVICE FROM STRAYER AND PETERS BUSINESS SCHOOLS:

"There are four P's to business: 1---<u>Place</u>---location is vital. 2---<u>Personality</u>---you've got to be likeable. All sales is selling yourself. 3---<u>Product</u>---obviously, you have to provide a product that people want. 4---<u>People</u>---you've got to hire good people."

"At Strayer the teachers always repeated the PMA idea---Positive, Mental, Attitude. It's true in many areas of life, but definitely in business."

KELLY ON AMERICA:

"This is a very good country. If you want to start a business here you don't have to be born into a family that has done the same thing for hundreds of years. You can just buy a truck, make a plan, and hang your shingle."

"Americans are good, decent people for the most part. I just don't see why we keep electing such idiots to make our laws."

KELLY ON ATHENS:

"When I started here I had this old van with a worn-out muffler. You could hear it from miles away. People always knew when Kelly was coming."

KELLY ON PLANNING AHEAD:

"I remember once in Texas when I was working with my partner, we did this job and got paid $1000. He spent his money on crap, liquor, women. I put mine in the bank and put some back into the business. I own my own business today with two locations. He died a few years after we split up the business."

KELLY ON MANKIND'S RHYMING CRUELTY:

"Man to man is so unjust that you just don't know who to trust."

KELLY ON RETIREMENT:

"I'd be bored in fifteen seconds."

KELLY ON POLITICS:

"Politics didn't start on Earth. It started in Heaven. Satan tried to convince other angels to turn against God. That's politics."

KELLY ON DEATH AND LIFE AFTER DEATH:

"When I was working at the hospital, I saw people die. I saw that vapor, that last breath, that 'soul.' You can see a little puff of smoke, then there's just a chunk of meat lying there on the table."

"No one had ever come back and told us what's on the other side of the river."

"Once you're dead, you're gone off somewhere."

KELLY ON ANIMALS:

"The dogs and the cats, they don't talk, but sometimes they communicate better than the people."

KELLY ON MONEY:

"I didn't worry about money. I never have. If you have a dream and you pursue it, you can work it out and find the money. The dream's the thing."

KELLY ON PURSUING A DREAM:

(After pointing out the window to the parking lot of one of his restaurants) "That van right there represents a dream. It means that I didn't have to rent from U-Haul or Enterprise anymore. My dream was just sitting there at the Chevy dealer."

KELLY ON THE GOVERNMENT:

"The government doesn't like smart people. They're all afraid that you'll take their job."

KELLY ON TEAMWORK:

"Two heads are better than one. Three heads move mountains. Four heads can take you to the stars."

WHAT THE HECK IS ACKEE?

According to *Webster's Dictionary,* ackee (also 'akee') is "the fruit of an African tree (*Blighia sapida*) of the soapberry family grown in the Caribbean area, Florida and Hawaii for its white or yellowish fleshy aril that is edible when ripe but is poisonous when immature or overripe and that has a toxic pink raphe attaching the aril to the seed."

Yeah, I don't know what 'raphe' or 'aril' are either, but I do know that ackee goes great with saltfish.

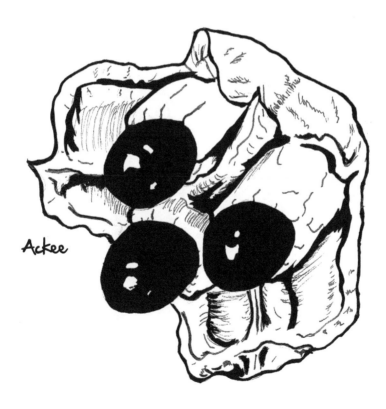

Ackee

I'VE AIDED IN A LOT OF BIRTHS, ACCIDENTALLY

I was going to put up a poster of baby pictures in one of my restaurants. My plan was to tape these pictures of newborns onto some poster board, hang it on my wall, and label the display, "MY BABIES." I still might do it…but I can't shake the thought that customers would assume that it was a poster with all of my illegitimate kids on it.

The truth is that pregnant women, when they're nearing the end of their nine-month cycle, often crave spicy foods. I've been told that spicy foods actually help in the birth, pushing the kids out. I can only assume that the babies want to be born so that they can cut out the middleman and eat my Jerk Pork.

CPSIA information can be obtained
at www.ICGtesting.com
Printed in the USA
FFHW021056141119
56054517-62025FF